MISSING!

The Disappeared, Lost or Abducted in Canada

Lisa Wojna

QUAGMIRE
PRESS

SEP 0 4 2008

The Publisher: Quagmire Press Ltd.
Website: www.quagmirepress.com

Library and Archives Canada Cataloguing in Publication

Wojna, Lisa, 1962–
   Missing : the disappeared, lost or abducted in Canada / Lisa Wojna.
Includes bibliographical references.

ISBN 13: 978-0-978340-90-2
ISBN 10: 0-978340-90-6

   1. Missing persons—Canada. I. Title.

HV6762.C3W65 2007   362.8   C2007-904190-6

Project Director: Lisa Wojna
Project Editor: Kathy van Denderen
Cover Image: Courtesy of Photos.com / © 2007 JupiterImages Corporation
Photo Credits: Every effort has been made to accurately credit the sources of
photographs. Any errors or omissions should be reported directly to the pub-
lisher for correction in future editions. Photographs courtesy of Sergeant
Michel Fournier, RCMP Forensic Artist (p. 239, DSCN2525, Face04);
Ontario Provincial Police Resolve Initiative (p. 241, P20060144_01,
P20060144_02; p. 245, P20050028_02, P20050028_05; p. 247,
P20060042_02; p. 249, P20050001_6, P20050001_7, P20050001_8);
Glendene Grant (p. 262, Jessica Foster); Lucy Glaim (p. 263, Delphine Nikal;
p. 264, Cecilia Nikal).

PC: P5

 Canadian   Patrimoine
Heritage   canadien

Contents

Dedication

In memory of all those who have gone missing over the years. May there be answers and closure for everyone mourning their absence.

Acknowledgements

Tackling a subject like missing persons is like writing about a ghost. Much of the time the information culled from quite literally thousands of sources was necessarily circumspect. Key factors, especially in ongoing investigations, are often withheld from the public—many of the cases covered within these pages remain unsolved, thus still open. And countless times I've found myself rummaging through conflicting "facts." To say my research options were limited is an understatement. I can only pray that some small semblance of justice was paid to each of the missing persons and their loved ones covered in these pages.

At this point in my writing career, I've penned several books, none of which could have been possible without considerable assistance from sources, editors, publishers and readers along the way. But never has this been truer than with this project. Without the folks who were willing to talk, adding what they knew about one particular case or another, some of these stories would have been left out. Without questions and prodding by others I've spoken to, certain topics would have never been tackled. And without a lot of people taking time out of their busy workdays to dig up pictures or proof stories, what follows would have been considerably less thorough. Thank you to everyone—you all know who you are. Any errors or omissions in the stories that follow are, without a doubt, mine. In advance, please accept my deepest apologies should that be the case.

In particular, I'd like to thank the following:

The Wetaskiwin Public Library for their ongoing support; Kat Strachan for patience with a newbie; Glendene Grant for opening your heart when your pain is still so very raw; Lucy Glaim for revisiting the tragedy of two missing relatives; Mark Bonokoski for answering a cold-call email with such grace and speed; public relations manager Theresa Brien; Tony Romeyn and the Doors of Hope; Lisa Krebs and the Highway of Tears; Councilor Rena Zatorski of the Lheidli T'enneh Nation; and Amnesty International Canada. As well, the following law enforcement officials made time in their busy schedules—where they are dealing with far more important issues than my constant prodding—to help with this project, thank you so very much: Constable Kelly West, Constable Kirk Chiasson, Detective Constable Douglas Dyke, Acting Sergeant Carole Lafleur, Detective Steve Mackey and Constable Wayne Oakes.

Thank you so very much to my editor, Kathy van Denderen. I am so eternally grateful that I landed such a talented, sharp-eyed editor. Your insight and care for detail has taken my initial draft, warts and all, and helped craft it into the book it became. And it was wonderful to work with someone who was as earnest as I when it came to honouring the memories of these missing persons and their loved ones.

Thank you, as always, to dear Faye. Your constant support and endless patience with my ongoing neurotic worries on everything I do is appreciated so much more than words can ever express. I'm so very glad to have a mentor like you.

And last, but certainly not least, to my beloved family. To my parents, Mary and Michael Wojna. To my longsuffering husband Garry, who supports everything I do with rarely a complaint. To my wonderful adult children: Peter, Melissa, Matthew and Alex. And to my darling and precocious two-year-old Jada, who spent many long hours working beside Mama, content to write make-believe books of her own as long as she could remain close by. I love you and thank you all from the bottom of my heart. Without you all, this and anything else I do would be meaningless.

Introduction

My mother was a true-crime nut long before it became popular. As a youngster, I recall her reiterating all the latest horror stories from around the world on an all too regular basis. She usually picked up these twilight zone tidbits from newspapers and magazines she'd read or some radio segment she heard. Many of her stories gave me nightmares and are quite likely where at least some of my neurotic tendencies stem from.

Truthfully, though, the fear she instilled in me wasn't completely without its benefits. I remember hitchhiking once (Sorry, Mum!) with a friend along Winnipeg's Narin Avenue at a time when, aside from the Starlight Drive-In and a couple of industrial sites, it was a lonely, vacant stretch of road. It was dark, but peering into the car that stopped for us, the elderly fellow offering us a ride seemed harmless enough. When we got in, though, alarm bells were pealing loudly, and I was watching for the next red light. The white-haired gent behind the wheel wasn't dressed in what I thought an appropriate manner for a respectable senior. He wore clunky, garish jewellry, much too much white for my liking, and the interior of his car was uphol-stered in red velvet. I don't think he appreciated it when my friend and I jumped out of the car as it stopped for a red light, but I didn't trust him. Maybe Mum's words of warning saved me from facing a fate similar to some of the young girls whose stories you are about to read.

Somehow, out of the entire repertoire of horror stories Mum so delighted in sharing, what grips my heart with fear like nothing else is the thought of someone close to me going miss-ing. What if Dad went on his annual hunting trip and disap-peared? What if someone abducted my baby sister, and we never saw her again? What if one of my children vanished? A disap-pearance is so wrapped in mystery and potential trepidation that the mere thought of it is paralyzing to me. So when I set out to research this book, I knew it would be a life-changing experi-ence—and it was.

The stories that follow are tragic and devastating, it is true. And I've learned about things my scariest nightmares couldn't have conjured up. (Just read a few stories on the media coverage of the Pickton trial, and in five minutes you'll be changed forever.) But the stories herein also speak of incredible human resilience. They speak of indestructible hope. Of hero-ism. Of bravery. Of courage. In my research, I've heard about reunions years after authorities have thought the missing person dead. I've also spoken with mothers who refuse to give up hope. And I've come across stories of abducted youth who've survived unspeakable abuse, such as the story of 13-year-old Jessyca Mullenberg of Wisconsin. This young woman trusted a writing coach and left with him one Saturday morning under the guise of meeting with a publisher for a project she'd been working on. She fell asleep in the car, only to wake to find herself bound and gagged and her captor telling her she was now his "daughter," and she'd do as he said, otherwise he'd murder her and her family. It was almost four long months before she was rescued from the man who raped and brutalized her over and over again. She was a changed person, but she survived.

This world can be a very dangerous place indeed. We will never rid it of predators. But even in the darkest night, during the most unspeakable brutality, they will not win. If these stories are any indication, love and hope will continue to prevail. Against all odds.

Chapter One

What Is "Missing"?

For a loved one whose family member or friend has gone missing, the definition of "missing" is quite simple. The individual isn't where he or she usually is at any given time, hasn't called in a while, hasn't shown up to work, hasn't been seen at home and no one can get in touch with that person. The behaviour is uncharacteristic at best, downright strange even. But what can we do about it?

Investigating a potential missing person's case is one of the most difficult situations law enforcement has to deal with. And if the missing person is an adult, that complicates matters significantly. It's not as simple as calling your local police or RCMP detachment, making a report and expecting instant action. After all, how do you really know someone has gone missing? Maybe Aunt Jess just took an extended vacation and forgot to tell you, her only living relative? Or maybe your favourite uncle planned an outing and was sure he'd informed you, but hadn't? And it's perfectly legal for an adult to choose to go missing. Perhaps this is what happened?

Although a fair amount of research has been conducted on the study of missing children in most developed countries around the world, a close look at the problem of missing adults isn't something that's been tackled with equal vigour, partly because of the aforementioned complexities involved. According to the National Missing Persons Helpline, research in the United Kingdom suggests that of the 210,000 missing persons cases reported each year in that area, most return safe and sound within 72 hours. An Australian Mental Health Association paper entitled *Someone Is Missing—An Emotional Resource for Family and Friends of Missing Persons* points out that of the 30,000 Aussies who go missing there during any given calendar year, "about 99.5 percent are located, often within a month from the time of disappearance." And in Canada, a 2005 consultation paper prepared by the Policing, Law Enforcement and Interoperability Branch of Public Safety and Emergency Preparedness cites about 100,000 reports of missing persons in the country annually. Here again, most are discovered in short order. Still, there are those individuals who for whatever reason remain on the missing persons list a year after being reported missing—an estimated 4800, or almost five percent, according to the RCMP.

So what, exactly, is the definition of a "missing person"? The legal definition in an Australia paper commissioned by the

Missing Persons Unit and the Australian Bureau of Criminal Intelligence is "…anyone who is reported missing to police, whose whereabouts are unknown and where there are fears for the safety or concerns for the welfare of that person." Canada does not have a standard definition of a "missing person," but it is safe to say that, depending on the protocol of any particular detachment, law enforcement officials don't typically get involved until the person has been missing for between 24 and 72 hours, except when there are concerns for that person's safety. And because "concerns" is subjective, clear guidelines outlining intervention aren't something that to date have been uniformly designed.

As with any other police matter, the longer the time lapse between an event and the onset of an investigation, the more opportunity there is for a trail to get cold. It's one of the many concerns families of missing loved ones regularly point out as a problem when it came to initiating an investigation in their respective situations. Still, if law enforcement went full throttle on every missing person's case, they'd not have time for other pressing matters.

How to deal with the investigation of missing persons is also a spiderweb of complexity. If the "why" is known in any given case, clearer links can be made and a better plan of action developed to locate that person. Unfortunately, knowing why someone vanished without a trace is usually a mystery until the case is resolved.

One step to dealing effectively with missing adults is the formation of a centralized, national clearinghouse where information about missing, at-risk and endangered adults can be easily accessed by the public as well as law enforcement and the media. It's something the family of Fran Young has long been advocating. Their 36-year-old daughter decided to take an evening walk in her Kitsilano neighbourhood in Vancouver on April 6, 1996. She was never seen again, and her family has been looking for her ever since. Through a website they've created about their missing daughter, they are encouraging Canadians to petition the federal government towards developing this type of search tool. Visit www.findfran.com for more information on how you can become involved.

Being proactive is one way many families cope with the grief of having a loved one go missing. Although their efforts haven't always brought their loved one home, they have produced results for other families. Such is the case of Susana Trimarco de Veron of Argentina. Since her 23-year-old daughter, Marita, was kidnapped in San Miguel de Tucuman on April 3, 2002, Susana has walked through often dangerous neighbourhoods and alleyways looking for information on her daughter's whereabouts. In doing so, she stumbled into the world of human trafficking where victims like her daughter—frequently women and young girls but certainly not exclusively—have been snatched, often in broad daylight, held against their will and exploited through prostitution or other forms of slavery. It's a profitable underground activity and far more common than we might want to believe in our civilized world. Those involved don't take kindly to snoopy mothers disrupting their criminal enterprises. Yet despite false leads, death threats and other obstacles to her quest, Susana has helped 100 young women escape their forced bondage and find their way home. She was honoured as a Woman of Courage by U.S. Secretary of State Condoleezza Rice on March 8, 2007, but Susana has yet to find her daughter.

Although it may be surprising to learn that human trafficking actually exists and isn't merely fodder for fiction, other seemingly outrageous claims have also been blamed for disappearances. In the 1970s, a Canadian psychiatrist, Dr. Lawrence Pazder, took on a patient named Michelle Smith. Smith lived with her husband, a respected surgeon, and daughter in Victoria, BC, where Michelle was raised. During her therapeutic relationship with Dr. Pazder (which over a decade became intimate and eventually the two were married), Smith was helped to recover repressed memories from her childhood—memories that were hindering her in adulthood. If her allegations were true, it was amazing she was alive to speak of them.

In a book the couple eventually co-authored, called *Michelle Remembers*, the pair recounts tales of torture, abduction, deprivation, neglect, poisoning and being thrown into a car with a corpse, all in the name of satanic rituals. Smith alleged the ritualistic torture began when she was five years old. The book gained such notoriety that it was often referred to by religious institutions, the British child welfare lobby, law enforcement, social workers and, perhaps most importantly, the public, as an author-itative source on the matter. It earned its place as a bestseller with offers of a Hollywood movie deal and was credited with initiating a "ritual abuse" panic in Victoria and elsewhere.

Satanic cults have often been blamed for child abduc-tions, some people openly voicing their belief that children are often victims of abduction by a satanic cult. But could there pos-sibly be any truth whatsoever in such allegations? Michelle Smith's family vehemently argued against the claims she made in the book, and her father, Jack Roby, filed a Notice of Intent to sue should the publishers accept a film deal. The RCMP have gone on record as saying there has never been a prosecution in Victoria for satanic practices, and *Michelle Remembers* has been relegated to the fiction shelf. Still, some swear such a cult exists.

For prostitutes "walking track" (the streets in any given city claimed as the area where sex-trade workers stroll for johns) in cities across the country, a far more concrete reason for these women's diminishing numbers can be blamed—Canadian law. Although prostitution isn't illegal in Canada, exorbitant licens-ing fees in excess of $4000 a year, far surpassing that of any other business, make prohibitive the setting up of an escort agency or massage parlour that would keep sex-trade workers indoors and safe. As well, anyone applying for that type of licence must undergo a criminal record check. If they've ever been picked up for soliciting on the street, which is where they go if they can't afford a licence, they can't work on the inside.

And if the cases of missing sex-trade workers in Edmonton and Vancouver and elsewhere are any examples, having to work on the street and getting into a john's car to go to an unknown location is a huge factor in their disappearance.

"I was down in Calgary for the (Jessie Foster) fundraiser and went out to check track and there was no one there," said Kat Strachan, an off-street out-call sex worker in Edmonton. "It was almost non-existent because Calgary lowered their licensing fees. It's only $40 down there."

Kat is one voice trying to get laws changed so that sex-trade workers can get off the street and work in a safer environment, thereby eliminating the victims in that demographic. Kat has given an affidavit to the Ontario Superior Court of Justice, outlining the cases of missing and murdered prostitutes in Alberta, as well as some of the situations she herself has faced. She's hoping her efforts will help revise federal solicitation laws so that sex-trade workers will no longer be charged for solicitation in public or the operation of a common bawdy house, and that living off the avails of prostitution will no longer be a criminal offence.

Changing the law is one way to protect some facets of society from predators. Another is public awareness. Erecting large billboards warning against hitchhiking along northern British Columbia's Highway 16 from Prince George to Prince Rupert and finding safer ways for their youth to travel are other options First Nations leaders in that area are looking at implementing to keep their young women safe. More than 30 women, and all but one of these women are of Aboriginal heritage, have disappeared along that stretch of road now commonly referred to as the "Highway of Tears." Feeling largely ignored by non-Native law enforcement officials, the Aboriginal community has charged that the cases of their missing children weren't taken seriously until recently. Today, Aboriginal leaders are taking action to advocate for the safety of their youngsters by hosting events such as the Highway of Tears Symposium, and Take Back the Highway marathon, which saw concerned citizens walk the more than 800-kilometre stretch from Prince Rupert to Prince George.

All these efforts and many others not mentioned will hopefully weave together to form a safety net for all our loved ones. Knowing that there are predators in our midst, sometimes in our own backyard, isn't something that should propel us to obsess in irrational fear, but it is a reality we can't ignore.

So, what is a missing person? For the purpose of this book, the definition of a "missing person" will mirror most closely that of Australia's National Advisory Committee on Missing Persons: Someone is considered missing when you are concerned because you are unable to locate that person. Individuals go missing for any number of reasons: they've been abducted, had an accident or have chosen to disappear for their own reasons. This book examines missing persons cases in each of these, and other, scenarios. In absolutely every story, I seek to honour the missing individuals and their families, and at the very least, to help those struggling with just such a situation to know they are not alone.

Chapter Two

Long Gone, Never Forgotten

What a person experiences when a loved one goes missing is, for most of us, beyond comprehension. The agony and helplessness that is felt must be unimaginable. Hope, though thin, is the only straw to grasp. And as time wears on, that hope evolves from a desire for a happy reunion to the need for answers, however grim. At what point, if ever, is hope replaced with a solemn resignation that answers might never be forthcoming—at least not in this lifetime? On the one hand, we may argue, we have to be realistic. After all, in reality, what are the chances, after an extended period of time has passed, that a missing loved one is still alive? On the other hand, reports of missing persons turning up decades later aren't unheard of.

For Raymond Power Jr., who was profiled on *America's Most Wanted* television series, seven months of wandering the streets of Chicago, Illinois, homeless and unsure of who he was came to an end when another man at the shelter where he was staying decided to help his new friend discover his true identity. Although details are sketchy, the resident of New York disappeared in the fall of 2005 and had been basically living in an amnesiac state ever since. He was reunited with his family in February 2006.

Even more bizarre was the East Texas–area rescue of Bobbi Louaine Parker in April 2005. Also profiled on *America's Most Wanted*, the wife and mother of two had disappeared 10 years earlier and had been held captive against her will by convicted killer and escaped prisoner Randolph Dial. Dial had kept Bobbi away from the general public, living in a trailer on a wooded lot, and he threatened to kill her family if she attempted an escape. She was discovered after Dial was recaptured in Campti, Texas, in April 2005.

So when does a person give up hope? The answer, of course, is unique to each individual. But in reality, when you love someone, hope never completely dies. ∽

LONG TIME GONE

On one hot and dusty morning in July 2006, Cal Schroyen of JBA Petroleum thought the day would be much like any other. Pull the pants on one leg at a time and get to work. He'd be digging up a couple of old fuel tanks near a convenience store in Saskatoon's Sutherland area. Routine work, really. Or so he thought.

During the process of the excavation, Cal noticed something odd roll out into the dirt. "It seemed a little unusual so we picked it up and had a look at it, and it turned out to be a human skull," Cal told *W-FIVE* reporters. As soon as he realized what he'd discovered, Cal called police. Immediately the area was cordoned off, and so began the process of unearthing whatever other clues the cavernous hole held. It took three days of careful digging before excavation of what turned out to be an old abandoned well was completed and the contents of the makeshift grave revealed—the complete skeletal remains of a woman, her clothing, a gold chain, parts of a barrel and assorted other items.

University of Saskatchewan forensic archeologist Ernest Walker determined the remains were that of a "healthy Caucasian woman, 25 to 35 years of age and a metre-and-a-half [5 feet] tall." Clothing and textile experts dated the garb she was wearing as current to between 1910 and 1920. Back then, Saskatchewan was an untapped wilderness, and new settlers in the province were in for many years of hard labour before they'd see much return from the soil they tilled. For the women following their menfolk, life could prove particularly cruel. A sod shack to call home, and chopping wood and hauling water to cook a meal or wash the laundry wasn't something their previous life in England or thereabouts prepared them for. And judging by the quality of the gold chain discovered with this woman's remains, it seemed that at some point in her life she'd had a somewhat genteel existence. Because it appeared that the unknown woman had been locked away in a barrel and hidden from sight, even the most scrupulous of us has to wonder if she came to this land of opportunity only to be murdered.

Using the 1910–20 time frame as reference, investigators began culling through old news reports, looking for stories about missing women. The woman's body was so well preserved, thanks to a mixture of gas and water that created a wax-like substance called adipocere, that investigators were able to extract mitochondrial DNA samples. News of the discovery was put out through the media, and people were asked to revisit their family stories of missing female relatives. Should a plausible connection surface, DNA would confirm an identity. Although as of this writing this woman's identity has yet to be determined, anxious individuals with stories of missing relatives from the past were eager to provide blood samples to test for a match.

If date estimates are correct, this young woman went missing almost 100 years ago, and her remains only discovered recently. If this story, being dubbed Canada's oldest cold case, is any indication, a missing family member affects his or her descendants generations later. So how long does one hope for an answer on the disappearance of a loved one? The answer is, quite possibly, for as long as it takes. ∞

HISTORY REPEATS ITSELF

When Jack Robertson moved the family's auto dealership, Robertson Motors, to its Danforth Avenue location, in Toronto, Ontario, in 1943, he knew he'd chosen a prime location for his thriving business. Since its incorporation back in 1938, Robertson Motors had outgrown its previous home, and the Danforth address would give Jack plenty of room for the company's current inventory and a lot of opportunities to expand as it continued to prosper.

And expand it most certainly did. In 1949 a new cement pad was laid, and business continued to boom. Robertson Motors went on to sell and repair vehicles for the next 55 years, employing in its ranks several of the Robertson clan before closing up shop in 1993. Two years later, the building and the cement pad that anchored it to its Danforth home faced the wrath of a wrecking ball. Breaking up the cement floor was heavy work, and a large backhoe was used for the job.

Workers gathered at the job site had a lot more to chew on than their suppers on the night of Thursday, May 18, 1995. Earlier on in the evening, as the backhoe was making progress on the cement pad, a metal barrel was uncovered, along with the skeletal remains of a woman. Police were called, and an investigation immediately commenced, bringing with it the expertise of anthropologist Dr. Jerry Melbye. At that point Dr. Melbye was affiliated with the University of Toronto and had worked with the Centre of Forensic Sciences in the past. It was his job to supervise the excavation, ensuring proper care would be taken and every available clue uncovered. In addition to the skeleton, a shoe and pieces of women's clothing were found, along with reddish-coloured hair. The woman was also wearing an upper dental plate, and police were hopeful that dental records would assist in identifying her.

At first the unknown woman was thought to be in her teens or early 20s, but as more clothing was uncovered, and experts went on to examine the skeletal remains, it was determined she was much older—perhaps even in her 30s or 40s. If that was true, the woman couldn't be one of three teens who'd gone missing in the 1950s on three different occasions and who have never been recovered. Specialists also pegged the unknown woman's height at between 166 and 172 centimetres (between 5 feet 5 and 5 feet 7 inches).

Armed with this new information, police began digging through old files. With several changes in the structure of area police departments since the late 1940s, just finding these files was a challenge. By now it was clear that the victim uncovered at the old automotive site was murdered, and such a discovery has a way of quieting voices that may have otherwise come forward with information.

Still, a few tips did trickle in. And police uncovered one old report of 35-year-old Isabelle Trache who left home on January 15, 1949, leaving behind seven children, the youngest of whom was only one year old. But none of the tips panned out. Isabelle is still missing, and the woman buried under a concrete slab is still unnamed.

If the preceding two stories seem to be extremely rare, think again. Sadly, perpetrators covering up their misdeeds by burying their victims aren't as uncommon as you would think. A Google search of something as obscure as "body in barrel" brought up 8630 entries one day in April 2007. Among the results was a story reported by the *New York Times* of a woman between 25 and 30 years of age who'd been murdered and buried in a steel drum under a Long Island home in 1969. She was discovered in September 1999. Her identity was later confirmed as that of a young Hispanic woman who'd worked for the property owner's plastics company and was believed to have become pregnant by him. The man committed suicide just 20 hours after being questioned about the discovery.

In January 2004, the *Sunday Mirror* posted a story of a man who'd been bound, gagged and brutally murdered. He'd been found covered in plastic and near a barrel he'd almost certainly been stuffed into, floating in the water at the base of a 180-metre cliff near East Sussex in England. Police there looked into the possibility that the victim had been dumped by a passing ship. And in April 2004, the *Oakland Tribune* reported a disturbing story about a fire that had destroyed the family home of 49-year-old Annette Lusk and claimed the lives of her 84-year-old father and his 85-year-old girlfriend. Lusk was told that a body discovered in a barrel located in what remained of her father's garage was that of her long-lost mother, Francis Adams, who'd disappeared almost 30 years earlier. Imagine wrapping your head around that one!

The list is endless. It's almost enough to make you wonder about the possible mysteries buried beneath the ground you
walk on. ∾

JOY AND SORROW

When Sheldon and Helen Crumback pulled out of their Toronto
driveway and headed to Detroit for the weekend of May 27,
1950, they did so without any hesitation. The wedding they
were about to attend was going to be a joyous affair, and the
Crumbacks were looking forward to reconnecting with old friends
and distant relatives. The trip would also provide a little getaway
for the couple, since their three children weren't with them.

Their middle youngster, 13-year-old Bruce, was planning to overnight at a friend's house. That left Mabel, 19, and
eight-year-old Gary to fend for themselves at home. The senior
Crumbacks had no qualms about leaving Gary in Mabel's care
for the few days they'd be away. Mabel had always been reliable
and responsible, a typical first child in almost every way—an
adult pleaser, rule follower, high achiever and occasionally bossy.
She had an office job at the Eastern Steel Co., earning herself
the princely sum of $28 a week. Mabel was also an active mem-
ber of St. John's Baptist Church, singing at the church choir and
taking part in much of the church's social opportunities. Overall, Mabel would make any parent proud.

Still, she was a teenager, after all, and a weekend alone must have felt like an indulgence for both Mabel and her little brother. Chances are Mabel wouldn't mind Gary staying up a little past his usual bedtime, and Gary wouldn't complain about Mabel having her beau over for a visit.

On Saturday, after an earlier, vigorous game of tennis, Mabel's boyfriend, Jim Bryan, called around for part of the evening. By his accounts he left Mabel's home at 12:30 AM that Sunday—a story that appeared to be upheld by at least one neighbour. But on Sunday morning, Gary awoke to an empty house. Thinking his sister had gone for a walk, he settled in to watch morning cartoons, glad to be able to monopolize the television set. As the day wore on, and his stomach complained louder and louder for food, he thought better of waiting for his sister to make his lunch and helped himself to whatever he could dig out of the refrigerator. At this point sources differ slightly. Several accounts have Jim returning to Mabel's house Sunday afternoon for dinner, only to discover through Gary that she was nowhere to be found. Another account has young Gary alone until his parents arrive back from Detroit just before midnight on Sunday. In any case, the police were called, Mabel's disappearance reported and an investigation started.

Since Gary was in bed through the night, Jim was admittedly the last person known to have seen Mabel. But Jim left the Crumback residence not long after midnight and, Gary, according to his story, had heard men's voices talking with Mabel long afterwards. Neighbours walking past the residence around 2:00 AM reported hearing a commotion as well. They also said they saw a light on in Mabel's bedroom around that same time, along with the Crumbacks' side door slightly ajar.

A search of the house didn't turn up much in the way of evidence. Nothing was amiss, and the only items not accounted for were Mabel's pyjama top and possibly a skirt. Her pyjama bottoms were neatly folded under her pillow, and her purse was left untouched in her room. She'd apparently put her hair up in curlers before retiring for the night, as they, too, were missing. But nothing of value had been taken from the rest of the house.

Media outlets across Ontario reported the story of the missing teen. Hundreds volunteered their services in search efforts, and for a time tips trickled in, most of which resulted in nothing more than innuendo. Someone reported seeing a girl who seemed to match Mabel's description in the back seat of a car, but the girl looked as though her hair had been dyed and she had been drugged. One tipster claimed to have seen her body strewn across a haystack. Under hypnosis, another individual described the area where Mabel's body was supposedly buried. Neither these nor any other bits of information turned over to police amounted to the discovery of even a shred of evidence.

For everyone concerned, it was as if Mabel Crumback vanished into thin air. Nothing made sense. No matter how deeply detectives dug into Mabel's life, they couldn't find the slightest indication she was in any trouble, had any enemies or had any reason to leave voluntarily. The house hadn't coughed up a single lead, either. There was no evidence of a struggle and no evidence that robbery could have been the motive. Should you be the type of person who believes in the existence of a parallel universe, it was as though Mabel walked through her bedroom door and into another dimension, never again to return to life as she knew it.

Throughout the years, any time there was a discovery of skeletal remains appearing to be that of a young woman, the case was re-examined. To date, though, nothing concrete has ever been discovered.

Over 50 years have passed since Mabel's mysterious disappearance. Despite the tragedy, life has a way of continuing on. The Crumbacks will have travelled through the many other milestones that life is certain to dish out. Children marry, and grandchildren are born. And people die. Helen and Sheldon Crumback passed away in 1983 and 1984, respectively. Perhaps they now know in death what they could never discover in life—the mystery of what became of their beloved Mabel. ❧

MASKED BANDIT

We've all heard various renditions of the lovers' lane legends. You know, the one where a couple sneak away for a little private time only to nearly lose their lives when confronted by a madman. The legends may be a welcome tool to parents eager to warn their daughters against such shenanigans. To youngsters, however, the stories are taken as little more than hot air. Either way, as is often the case, there's usually at least a smidgen of truth behind these kinds of tales. It's something to think about when reading through this next story.

~

By all accounts, Marion Joan McDowell was a force to be reckoned with in 1953. At just 17, the young Toronto-area teen knew well what she wanted in life and wasn't afraid to go out and get it. She'd been working since she was 15 years old, taking on jobs in retail and then in a bank before landing her last position as a typist for a printing company.

Hardworking though she was, Marion was not all work and no play. She loved sports, frequenting tennis courts, swimming pools and the like. And she had a fondness for nice, polite gentlemen, such as 19-year-old Jimmy Wilson. Although nothing came of the couple's meetings that summer, Marion bumped into the scaffold-rigger in early December, and the two went out on a date. One date led to another, and then another, and on December 6 the couple decided to take a ride to a quiet country road just a few kilometres into Scarborough. The spot was known as a meeting place for young couples. A kind of lovers' lane, if you will. And after a cigarette or two and a bit of small talk, they got a little cozy. Nothing heavy, mind you. Just a little bit of harmless necking. About an hour and a half after the couple parked the car, the door on Jimmy's 1942 Plymouth Coupe flew open. Shocking though it was, at first the couple wasn't concerned with the masked man standing by the driver's door, pointing a gun and demanding money. Jimmy explained to investigators that he and Marion thought the masked man was just someone playing a trick. As bizarre as this may seem, apparently such teasing wasn't uncommon. But then the masked man ordered Jimmy to get out of the car, and the sickening rush of fear must have gripped both youngsters.

Once he handed the bandit his wallet, which contained nothing more than a $10 bill, Jimmy's world turned black. Hit twice on the back of the head, he was knocked out. The next thing he remembered was being in a daze, floating in and out of consciousness, but he recalled lying in the back seat of his own car with Marion's bloody body strewn on top of him and the strange masked man driving them away. When they came to a stop, Jimmy roused enough to see the masked man dump Marion's body into the trunk of another car and drive away.

What to do? If Jimmy, in his hazy state, followed the alleged perpetrator and cornered him, he'd be in no condition for a standoff. He chose the only other option open to him. Quickly hefting himself into the front seat, he rushed home to tell his parents what had happened. Once police heard what took place, a massive manhunt was launched, which included upwards of 2000 volunteers and two helicopters. Jimmy was led away to the hospital and received 17 stitches to his injured head. Because he was the last person to see Marion, it was only natural that some suspicion fell on him, but he submitted to a lie detector test and passed with flying colours. Other bits and pieces of evidence also seemed to corroborate Jimmy's story. His wallet was found discarded, and pools of blood were obvious both in Jimmy's car and at the attack site. In addition, the area where his car was transported was private property, accessed only after the gate lock had been broken and the chain cut. Police also noticed two sets of tire tracks and uncovered a bar of Sunlight soap.

Perhaps it was this last bit of evidence that stirred unkind suppositions among the public about what happened to poor Marion. "What on earth would two young folks be doing sitting in a car for almost two hours?" some asked. The thinly veiled undertones suggested that Marion, like many other young women of her day, may have succumbed to a botched abortion. In any case, her family was never granted the peace that closure brings. Despite tips trickling in through the years, and even the odd confession or two, the case of Marion's disappearance remains a mystery to this day. ❧

THE SEARCH FOR ANSWERS

When news hit that human remains, which included part of a jawbone and at least a few teeth, were reportedly found west of Calgary's Pinebrook Golf Course in May 2000, Shelley Sawatzky cried. It was both welcomed and dreaded news for the young woman who, for most of her life, had been working to track down her birth mother Marguerite Peterson. Was there really an answer in sight?

Thirty-one-year-old Marguerite Peterson's abandoned vehicle was discovered just east of Canmore near an area called Dead Man's Flats on September 16, 1973. Everything inside the car was intact. Her purse lay in plain view. Her keys were even in the ignition. But there was no sign of Marguerite. Initial investigation into the disappearance revealed that Marguerite had purchased a .303 rifle on September 10, and it, too, was nowhere to be found. Although traces of the missing woman were never discovered, nor the rifle, her disappearance was ruled a suicide.

Fast-forward to 1982. Shelley Sawatzky is a young woman of about 21 in search of a mother she'd lost track of over the years. At the age of two, Shelley had been adopted, but her mother continued to visit from time to time until Shelley turned 11. Suddenly, the visits stopped with no explanation.

Typically, parents tend to be protective of their young, but perhaps Shelley's adoptive parents really didn't know why Marguerite stopped visiting. Either way, driven by a natural curiosity and the almost innate drive we all have to find answers to puzzling questions, Shelley embarked on a personal journey to shed some light on what happened to her birth mother. What she discovered while reading RCMP reports from the day confused her. The reports had Marguerite working as a cocktail waitress and dancer, and her associates as being of questionable characters. But that description didn't coincide with Shelley's knowledge of her mother, nor did it jive with the papers she came in possession of in 1993. According to that information, Marguerite was a secretary, had worked both in the oil and gas industry and with a law firm, and was even a certified pilot. The confusion as to her history may have come as the result of her driving taxi for a time for Shelley's birth father, since he was the one who had connections to a nightclub.

Shelley also learned that her birth mother had dreams of becoming a clothing designer and had enrolled in classes at Mount Royal College to begin the fall she went missing. The more Shelley dug, the more questions she unearthed. Nothing made sense to her. And although she was willing to admit suicide may have been a possibility for her mother's disappearance, the facts just didn't add up.

When Marguerite's car was discovered, about 20 police officers descended into the area. They came up empty-handed—no body, no rifle, nothing. Since 1973 a number of additional searches have taken place, including the one in May 2000. Unfortunately, the remains allegedly discovered by a passerby were not found again. Sadly, Shelley's questions remain unanswered because no evidence of her mother's plight has yet been recovered. ଐ

PRESUMED DEAD

Bright, brunette and beautiful—the black-and-white image of Crystal Elizabeth Van Huuksloot peering from the web pages of the Doe Network (an Internet database supplying information and photographs of individuals who'd been missing nine years or longer) beams and sparkles, emanating a warmth and radiance she must have surely displayed to those who knew her.

Crystal's story begins on a cool autumn day in October 1977 when she boarded a plane in Edmonton and flew to Toronto International Airport. Hers was a mission of mercy of sorts. Her boyfriend, Stacey Harris, appeared to have gotten himself into a little trouble with the law. He had been arrested on drug charges, and he called for Crystal to fly down with his bail money—all $15,000 of it, thank you very much. In a panic Crystal gathered what she could, about $3000, and stuffed it into a homemade money belt she strapped around her waist.

That she made it to Toronto is a proven fact. Records showed her visiting Stacey in the city's Don Jail. The meeting proved to be disheartening for Stacey when he learned Crystal had only been able to raise a portion of the money he needed. Not to worry, Crystal assured him. She had a plan. And when all her legitimate efforts to raise the funds didn't produce, Crystal is believed to have contacted a loan shark named Ian Rosenberg. At first it was thought that he promised her the money, but when it didn't come through, Crystal decided to fly back to Edmonton to see what she could do to raise the money.

Stacey likely didn't think twice when, during their last visit at the jail, Crystal informed him that Ian Rosenberg would be driving her to the airport. And so when she didn't arrive in Edmonton, the loan shark was questioned, and he admitted to dropping her off at the airport—but that's all he knew. However, flight records did not have her listed as a passenger, so even if he was being truthful, Crystal did not board the plane.

Seven months later, Ian and his girlfriend were shot and killed while still in bed. Police charged one of Ian's associates with the murders. They believed Ian knew of the suspect's involvement in Crystal's disappearance. But that individual was later acquitted because of a lack of concrete evidence.

It is quite possible that Crystal, in an effort to support her wayward lover, got herself mixed up with all the wrong people. But to this day, the murder of Ian and his girlfriend, and Crystal's disappearance, both remain unsolved.

Chapter Three

Highway of Tears

Trees. Lots of trees. A constant stream of aspen, spruce, cedar and assorted other evergreen and deciduous varieties make up much of what you'll see while driving along Highway 16 from McBride north to Prince George, BC. The sea of green lines the roadway thick and deep, disappearing into a wilderness so dense it's difficult to imagine how early explorers first traversed this unforgiving land—or how Canada's First Nations peoples carved a living for themselves here.

Today, aside from an eager logging industry that has left large chunks of the countryside remarkably anemic-looking, much of the 55 million hectares of forest covering the northern half of BC remains largely untouched by human development. Areas such as this section of road are so devoid of civilization that McBride provides motorists with their last chance to fill up with fuel before the 208-kilometre stretch leading travellers from that town to the great northern metropolis of Prince George. ∾

Smell is among our most powerful senses, and long before you notice the plumbs of smoke wisping into the sky beyond, you'll catch a whiff of the sulfur-like stink of rotten eggs. As you continue on, the odour gets stronger until, just a hill and a turn later, you come to Prince George. With a population of about 77,000, this northern city's survival is very much reliant on that sour scent. As BC's lumber industry grew, Prince George saw the development of several saw mills and pulp mills. By the 1970s, the manufacturing of pulp for the production of paper became increasingly important—an industry on which this northern community has become largely dependent.

Most of the folks who call northern BC their home live in Prince George. The rest are scattered among small communities dotting the winding highway to Prince Rupert and the Pacific coast in the west and Alaska in the north. With a relatively small population covering such a large parcel of land, residents are oddly independent yet reliant on each other. On the one hand, folks here tend to keep their own counsel. Communities are fairly tight-knit, and newcomers are often looked on as outsiders who need to prove themselves before they are accepted. On the other hand, the sheer remoteness of the north often thrusts people into circumstances where at times they're forced to reach out to strangers. Most often the Good Samaritan who meets their need is just that, a helpful soul lending a helping hand. Sadly, however, this is not always the case.

On a sunny day, regardless the season, there are few stretches of highway in the country that can compare with the beauty of Highway 16 from Prince George to Prince Rupert. For the residents of Smithers, their much loved Hudson Bay Mountain is the first majestic peak in an endless series that will lead travellers along the Bulkley River, past the thundering Moricetown Canyon and along the Skeena to the mouth of the ocean. The river is high in June, flooded with the mountains' spring runoff, and avid fisher folk take to the riverbeds in droves, searching for the year's first big catch.

In June, female bears cautiously emerge from their winter hideaways, baby cubs in tow, and meander down to the river looking for a feed of fresh fish. The leaves are just turning plump, ready to burst forth into summer's full foliage. Some residents plan their summer vacations while the rest of the town braces for the summer's tourist traffic. Plans for Smithers' annual folk festival, held over the summer solstice, are in full swing. Kids are excited about getting out of school and, in general, all is usually very good with the world. ∾

RAMONA WILSON

It was on such a day full of promise that 15-year-old Ramona Wilson ventured out to meet some friends. The vivacious high school student was full of youthful exuberance, excited about the coming summer, yet at the same time eagerly planning her future. She had dreams of becoming a psychologist, so school was a priority in her life. So was family. "Ramona was a bundle of joy, she made us all laugh, she was so young," her mother Matilda said in Sharmeen Obaid Chinoy's film documentary *Highway of Tears*, a project dedicated to this and several other disappearances along the stretch of highway that has since acquired the infamous title.

The last known sighting of Ramona was on June 11, 1994, when she was seen hitchhiking along the highway near Smithers. The community was still in upheaval over her disappearance when I moved to the area in December that same year. I remember her picture. Cliché or not, Ramona was truly a raven-haired beauty. What looked like a recent school photograph was centred on the countless missing person posters throughout the community, many strategically placed on shop doors. Each time I entered such an establishment, I couldn't help but pause for a moment, gaze at the sweet-looking youngster with the intense eyes and long, dark locks swept over one shoulder and wonder if there'd be a happy ending to what must have been a terrible nightmare for Ramona and her family.

In this case a happy ending was not to be. The following year Ramona's skeletal remains were discovered near the Smithers Airport. "They took the light of my life away from me," Matilda still mourns. What happened and the person responsible for her death remains a mystery to this day, but there's one thing Ramona's mother is very sure of: "The devil walks among us in so many ways." ∾

Delphine and Cecilia Nikal

Lucy Glaim works at the Office of the Wet'suwet'en in Smithers, BC. As a youth justice worker with the Wet'suwet'en Unlocking Aboriginal Justice program, it's Lucy's job to help build bridges and heal wounds inflicted through criminal or otherwise destructive behaviours. These wounds, to some degree, aren't unlike the pain Lucy herself has suffered on a daily basis since 1990. As the second oldest in a family of five children, Lucy was just 21 when her 15-year-old sister, Delphine Camillia Anne Nikal, disappeared. The last person known to have seen Delphine was a friend named Crystal, who noticed her hitchhiking to Telkwa from Smithers on June 14, 1990. When she didn't meet up with Crystal the next day, as was previously arranged, Crystal became concerned and called Delphine's family who, in turn, reported her missing.

"Delphine was a bright girl, full of life and didn't have a hard time saying what was on her mind. If she had an issue, she would deal with it up front and honestly," Lucy explained in an email correspondence. Like other young people, Delphine had her dreams. She wanted to continue on with her education after grade 12 and earn her teaching degree. "She loved young children…Delphine never missed a birthday of her young nieces and nephews and was always the bright centre of attention when she walked in the door," Lucy continues.

As of this writing, Delphine would have been 35 years old. Maybe she would have earned her teaching degree by now or opted for some other child-related career. Instead, the Nikal family mourns her loss and the loss of the children she almost certainly would have produced. She always wanted a family of her own to love and nurture. A bright, young voice is silenced, and even though it's closing in on two decades since she vanished, no one knows why, and her family remains in mourning.

"During the '90s we lived in a very racist town where we were doing our search ourselves because the RCMP didn't believe that Delphine was missing," Lucy said, remembering how she helped put up posters in malls and stores in Smithers, Houston and all the way to Granisle, about a 288-kilometre round-trip. "On our way back, we checked the malls to ask people if they had seen Delphine and discovered the posters had been ripped down."

~

That a family should never have to endure the torment of a missing child goes without saying. But the Nikal family had already experienced such a heart-wrenching scenario. One of the first cases listed on the string of missing persons associated with the Highway of Tears is that of Cecilia Anne Nikal, a cousin to the family. "Cecilia lived with her grandmother due to the fact that her parents were not healthy enough to raise a child at that time," Lucy said, adding that even with the best of intentions, Cecilia suffered abuse and was often bullied by neighbourhood kids.

Not much is known of her disappearance. According to the Nikal family, Cecilia was last seen in 1989 riding on the back of a motorcycle with a man who looked to be in his 30s, on Highway 16 near Smithers. Cecilia is one of the nine missing or murdered women listed on the Internet site called Highway of Tears, a Doors of Hope project. The website is dedicated to keeping the stories of these women who have disappeared along this stretch of road in the public eye, while at the same time providing support to family and friends.

Cecilia, however, is not currently one of the names on the RCMP's official list—a discrepancy seems to exist between opposing accounts of where she was last seen, and also because Lucy's sister, Roberta Cecilia Nikal, was at one point questioned by the RCMP. Because of the similar names, the RCMP believed they were questioning Cecilia when they were actually questioning Roberta. Angered by previous encounters with police and not realizing they should have been questioning her cousin, Roberta was insulted by their probing. The interaction ended up producing false information, and RCMP returned to the Nikal family saying Cecilia didn't want to be contacted when, all the while, Cecilia was still missing and had never been contacted.

Since a pattern of missing and murdered women along the Highway of Tears hadn't really been established at the time of Cecilia's and Delphine's disappearances, the Nikal family must have felt very alone in their search—particularly because it seemed that no one cared about their plight. Others would soon become more sympathetic, but that understanding would come with a high price tag. ∾

MORE MISSING WOMEN

No other women went missing for a few years, and perhaps the fear of what may have become of the Nikal cousins had subsided slightly. But all was not calm for long. In 1994, Ramona was the next to fall victim to the disturbing trend of missing women along Highway 16. Less than a month after her disappearance, on the July long weekend, 15-year-old Roxanne Thiara vanished. She'd been working as a prostitute in Prince George and apparently told a friend she was going out with a customer. It was the last anyone saw of her until her body was discovered the following month, on August 17. Since her last confirmed sighting, Roxanne had been somehow transported from Prince George to Burns Lake where her body was found dumped in a bush just a few kilometres east of town.

Another Prince George teen suffered the same fate as Roxanne just a few months later. The night of December 9, 1994, was supposed to be a time of celebration. The RCMP were hosting a Christmas dinner at the Prince George Native Friendship Centre on George Street, and 16-year-old Alishia Germaine had looked forward to attending the event. Alishia was known to struggle with drug use, and she supported herself at least partly through prostitution. Alishia's friends reported that she was trying to finish her education and build a new life for herself. The dinner likely spelled a little relief from her past and a hope for a brighter future. It was a hope she was robbed of later that same day when her body was discovered behind one of the city's elementary schools. She'd been murdered.

By now five young women had gone missing or were found murdered in just a few short years: Cecilia, Ramona, Delphine, Roxanne and Alishia. The level of fear throughout this stretch of BC's north was on the rise, especially among members of the Aboriginal community, and folks were starting to speculate that the deaths and disappearances were the work of a serial predator. Area law enforcement must have been considering the same possibility, because two FBI-trained profilers were seconded to the area for a week in 1995, the year after Alishia's body was discovered. But along with similarities in the cases, the psychological profilers must have noted as many differences, and the theory of a serial killer was abandoned— for a time. It would later resurface as a possibility in at least a few of the cases, but certainly not in all of them. ❧

LANA DERRICK

In the meantime, the family of Lana Derrick were entertaining unwelcome fears of their own. The 19-year-old forestry student at Terrace's Northwest Community College was heading home for the weekend of October 7, 1995. Studious, well liked, hardworking, dependable and trustworthy, Lana was the kind of daughter any parent would be proud of. So when she didn't make it to Hazelton, her hometown located 140 kilometres from Terrace, and then didn't show up for school the following Monday, red flags went up for everyone who knew her. She hasn't been seen or heard from since, nor has her body been recovered. Each year since her disappearance, after the warmer climes of spring thaws the snow-covered ground, the Derrick family, along with many of Lana's friends, gather together and search various stretches of remote roadways in the region hoping to discover what became of their loved one. ✣

Nicole Hoar

From 1995 until June 2002, residents along the Highway of Tears had a reprieve from their fear. There were no official reports of missing or murdered women during that time. But all that was about to change when Nicole Hoar, a 25-year-old resident of Red Deer, Alberta, working as a tree planter in the Prince George area, had a week off from work and decided to surprise her sister with an unannounced visit. Nicole's sister lived in Smithers, roughly 371 kilometres away from where Nicole was working. Friends reportedly dropped her off at a service station just outside Prince George. With no viable means of transportation, Nicole decided to hitchhike. It was Friday, June 21, 2002.

Summer solstice. A large contingent of Smithereens would be at their local fairgrounds, kicking up their heels in celebration of the town's annual Music Festival. It was an event that Nicole would have enjoyed attending, had she reached her destination. She never did.

Of all the missing and murdered women listed along the Highway of Tears before Nicole's disappearance and since, she was the only victim who was not at least partially of Aboriginal descent. It was Nicole's case, however, that added momentum to what was until that time largely a community-based groundswell of concern. The Highway of Tears Symposium Recommendation Report dated June 16, 2006, and penned by the Lheidli T'enneh First Nation, Carrier Sekani Family Services, Carrier Sekani Tribal Council, Prince George Native Friendship Centre and the Prince George Nechako Aboriginal Employment & Training Association, credits Nicole's disappearance for garnering more widespread media attention. The report goes on to point out, "Of most importance, the media and the general public became aware that Nicole Hoar's disappearance was not an isolated incident!"

The Hoar family maintained a public search for their daughter. The Hudson's Bay Company in Red Deer, where Nicole's father, Jack, was a long-time employee, established a $25,000 reward for information on Nicole's whereabouts. The reward raised the profile of the family's plight and resulted in hundreds of tips pouring into RCMP headquarters. One tip in particular turned out to be the last confirmed sighting of the young woman. In late July 2002, a man came forward saying he spoke with Nicole on the day of her disappearance. He stated that he and his children were driving west on Highway 16, noticed Nicole hitchhiking and stopped to pick her up. But when he discovered she was going to Smithers, considerably farther west than he was travelling, he decided against giving her a ride because he didn't want to leave her stranded midway to her destination. He suggested she wait for someone who was going the full distance.

Because of the ongoing flow of tips from the public on Nicole's case, it garnered far more search efforts than others in the area previously had. A *Calgary Sun* article dated July 14, 2002, reported that the RCMP had launched "one of the biggest ground and air searches ever in northern BC." Ditches along the highways in BC were scoured "by 66 professional search and rescue team members, backed by 200 volunteers, and…more than 50 tree-fellers and loggers from the reforestation service where Nicole worked."

Publicity was bolstered even more when Olympian Steve Elm and five other Canadian speed skaters held a fundraising meet at Calgary's Olympic Oval on July 13, 2002. A long-time friend of Nicole's, Steve had promised to break the 3000-metre world speed skating record. According to a *Calgary Sun* article dated July 14, 2002, Elm exceeded his own expectations with an unofficial time of 3:42.87—a full second under the official world record. The event drew the desired crowds and added $1800 in donations towards a trust fund that had been established to help pay for additional expenses in the search for Nicole.

Despite all the search efforts, media attention, a poster campaign that covered "every available post and pole from Prince George to Smithers," the resurfacing of FBI-trained psychological profilers and the best of the best of Canada's detectives descending on the scene, not a trace of the missing woman has ever been found. ∾

TAMARA CHIPMAN

Again, the highway fell silent for a time. Three uneventful years passed before another family was thrust into the unwelcome spotlight of the families grieving over their missing and murdered loved ones along the Highway of Tears.

A change of plans or mistaken communication, whatever the cause, it was three weeks before the Chipman family reported 22-year-old Tamara Chipman missing. She was last seen hitchhiking out of Prince Rupert late in the afternoon of September 21, 2005, and was thought to be making her way home to Terrace. But she was going through a troubled time and was facing charges for assault. Her family in Terrace didn't report her missing because initially they thought she was visiting relatives in the Lower Mainland, and then they thought she might be avoiding the law. Troubled as she may have been, it was uncharacteristic for Tamara not to call her father, Tom. When he returned home from fishing, a job that took him away from Terrace for long periods at a time, Tom expected he'd have a message or two on his answering machine waiting for him from his daughter. There was nothing. It was even more uncharacteristic of the young mother to be away from her little boy. A worried Tom called the police. It took another five days after she was reported missing by her family before the RCMP began actively investigating the case, but there was enough evidence linking Tamara's disappearance to others along the highway over the years to garner the help of 10 detectives, along with communications between Terrace and the major crimes unit in Prince George.

Despite relentless ground searches conducted by the Chipman family well into December, and ongoing investigations by the RCMP, evidence leading to Tamara's whereabouts remains, to date, elusive. ∽

AIELAH SARIC-AUGER

Aielah Saric-Auger was the last person to be added to the Highway of Tears missing and murdered. Her body was discovered on February 10, 2006, just east of Prince George. At the age of 14, Aielah had gone missing eight days earlier. Yet like Cecilia Nikal, Aielah's name is not on the official RCMP list linked to the highway, and the reasons for that discrepancy are not clear. Two other young women, however, are. Monica Ignas' partly nude body was discovered in a gravel pit near Terrace on April 6, 1975. She went missing the previous December, and an examination of her remains indicated she died as a result of strangulation. She was just 15. And on August 26, 1989, 24-year-old Alberta Gail Williams disappeared from Prince Rupert. Her body was also discovered, three weeks after her disappearance, about 37 kilometres east of Prince Rupert.

What was happening along the Highway of Tears, and who was responsible for the disappearance of these young, vibrant women? They came from different circumstances and experienced many of life's joys and sorrows to varying degrees. The only thing these 11 women uniformly had in common was their youth. Some folks in the region think the number of missing and murdered women is actually much higher—the Highway of Tears Symposium report suggests the number of victims is closer to 30.

There has been much speculation by area residents about what's really going on. Some swear by the theory that one or more serial killers are on the loose, pointing out that predators like Gary Leon Ridgway, the Green River killer, preyed for more than 20 years before being caught and ultimately confessing to the murder of 48 women between 1982 and 1998.

Although the RCMP doesn't believe a serial killer scenario is what they're looking at, they haven't completely ruled it out. "There is nothing to indicate there is a serial killer—nothing—but you can never close your mind to anything," Vancouver RCMP Sergeant John Ward said in a *Vancouver Sun* story dated November 26, 2005.

Since January 2006, a retired RCMP officer turned private investigator has been dedicating his time to digging for clues and collecting information in a bid to help find the person responsible for the years of carnage along the northern highway. To a large degree, Ray Michalko has not only dedicated his time but also his resources to the cause. Initially, he'd considered the possibility of a serial killer being responsible for most if not all of the reported cases. But his views have changed slightly. In October 2006, *The Smithers Interior News* reported Michalko as saying he had collected what he believed was good information on several of the cases and was working to verify some of it. "I think one person is involved in a couple murders or disappearances, but I don't think one person is responsible for all of them...I think it's just sort of a random act in some cases: somebody at the wrong place at the wrong time." For the people living in the pristine wilderness area, it's a horrific thought.

Just about any time of the year, even at the height of summer tourist season with its countless RVers touring Canada's northern wilderness, you can frequently stand on any portion of the almost 800-kilometre stretch of Highway 16 between Prince George and Prince Rupert and hear nothing more than your thoughts mingled with a bird call here and there and maybe a whisper of wind. Sometimes you can stand alone like that for several minutes, getting lost in the beauty of the world around you, before another vehicle passes by. But don't let that lull you into complacency. Danger could be lurking around the very next corner, in the very next vehicle.

Chapter Four

A Dangerous Life

"I picked prostitutes as my victims because I hate most prostitutes and I did not want to pay them for sex. I also picked prostitutes as victims because they were easy to pick up without being noticed. I knew they would not be reported missing right away, and might never be reported missing. I picked prostitutes because I thought I could kill as many of them as I wanted without getting caught."

—*Gary Ridgway, Green River Killer, convicted of murdering 48 prostitutes in the Seattle area over a two and one-half year period. He was a person of interest in several of the crimes as early as 1981 but wasn't successfully arrested until 2001, 20 years later.* ∾

GROWING PAINS

Life is really good at throwing us our share of ongoing challenges, and in the late 1990s, the breakup of our family as we
knew it has in many ways defined the young adults my children
are today. Coping skills are unique to every individual, and each
of my youngsters survived this family hardship differently.
Struggling myself, I hadn't realized how very vulnerable my
youngest son, Alex, was until it was too late to intervene and
save his innocence.

The beginning of the end for Alex started after I moved
my family to a new community. It was January 2000—a new
millennium and a new start, or so I hoped. I knew a move, especially one of more than 1500 kilometres, would be tough. But
for Alex, a 12-year-old trying to cope, a new home and new
school meant even more burdens to bear. Regardless how well
accepted he was, he felt ever the outsider. And despite being
named captain of his hockey team his first year on the ice in our
new community, he felt he was a failure. I knew he was having
a tough time of it. What I didn't know was how accurately predators can spot a troubled youth from miles away.

That's exactly what happened to Alex, who was approached
by an adult on his way home from school one day. Before too
long I'd received a call from another mother. "Did you know?"
she asked. I was floored. Together we spoke with our two sons,
who'd conspired to use a soda can to create a makeshift "bong"—
a water pipe used to enhance the pot-smoking experience.

Alex was just 13. How could he have a clue about drugs, much less creating a bong?

By then he was into far more than a little creative smoking. He'd been recruited to sell drugs in our new community, and although I wouldn't know it for years to come, he had already been working for dangerous felons. I would later also learn that one of these criminals, high on something pretty scary, held a 22-gauge shotgun to Alex's face, warning him what would happen should my little boy ever decide to cross him.

It took a long time before Alex broke free from the men who almost owned him for a while. And I thank God daily that our bout with the seamier side of life wasn't worse than it was. But he's been forever changed. His innocence lost. His look at life jaded.

~

For many women "walking track" across this country, childhood sexual abuse and drug addiction, such as the situations faced by my own son—people who work with troubled youth call these "risk factors"—landed them in their dangerous lifestyles. This is not an excuse. It is a reality.

In an *Edmonton Journal* article dated November 3, 2006, Kate Quinn, executive director for Prostitution Awareness and Action Foundation of Edmonton, estimated that about 500 women presently walk the streets in that city and make a living from prostitution, with as many as 10,000 men cruising those same streets to avail themselves of the services the women offer. Some of these women started prostitution as a way to flee horrible circumstances at home. Some of them are desperate to supplement their day jobs to pay the bills and feed their youngsters. Others have loving families who worry and pray, knowing their loved one is in perhaps the most dangerous profession around. Those families feel completely helpless to do anything, especially in light of the addictions, the pimps and the predators that imprison many prostitutes on the street.

Sometimes weeks or even months go by before these women are inclined to call home, so ashamed are they or paralyzed by fear that they'll be rejected by their families. This is likely why some sex-trade workers have just disappeared, and no one knows they are gone until the months drag on and Mom or Dad or a favourite sister finally gives up waiting for a phone call and calls the police. Their loved one is missing, or so they thought. By then family members often take the initiative to stroll track themselves, speaking with other street workers and looking and hoping to catch a glimpse of their family member. No one has seen her for a long time, they learn. How long? No one can recall. Drug addiction clouds the memory.

Edmonton's "track," the path in any community where those in the sex trade stroll, is along 118 Avenue. It's a dangerous stretch of road drawing a potentially deadly sort of clientele. It's a proven fact. A research paper prepared by the John Howard Society of Alberta in 2001 quotes 1997 statistics from the

Canadian Centre for Justice, pointing out that "63 prostitutes were murdered between 1991 and 1995. Of the 63, 50 were killed by johns, eight by pimps or in drug-related incidents and the remainder by husbands, common-law spouses and boyfriends."

Law enforcement officials and streetwalkers in Alberta's capital city don't need statistics to know that these women are in danger. Project KARE, a 2003 RCMP initiative that works in partnership with Edmonton Police Service, and Criminal Intelligence Service Alberta are currently looking into the more than 70 murders and disappearances of women involved in high-risk lifestyles, such as prostitution. And those are just the cases Project KARE is willing to go public about.

On January 21, 2005, Edmonton-area residents heard about a woman who needed to be included in the missing persons list. RCMP turned to Edmontonians with photographs and a media release that described 27-year-old Corrie Ottenbreit, a scant 55-kilogram (120-pound), blue-eyed redhead who looked much taller than her 166-centimetre (5-foot 5-inch) frame. She's smiling in the press release photograph, her long hair hanging straight down her back and a scarf flung over one shoulder. To look at her, she appears timid and a little gaunt, but it's hard to tell. And aside from profiling her physical description and what she was wearing when last seen, neither the press release nor subsequent news articles say much about the woman.

The last known sighting of Corrie was on May 9 the previous year—sometimes the police, in these types of cases, are reluctant to issue missing persons bulletins too soon since it's not uncommon for women engaged in prostitution to drop out of sight for a time, trying to hide from a threatening pimp or bad john or to perhaps work their way out of the business. In Corrie's case, neither friends nor family members, some of whom live in the Edmonton area, had heard from her since that last recorded sighting. Concern for her welfare was growing.

Police had another reason for concern. Rachel Quinney, another sex-trade worker, was found murdered one month after Corrie disappeared. Although RCMP spokesperson Corporal Wayne Oakes told *Edmonton Sun* reporters they hoped Ms. Ottenbreit had merely removed herself from life on the street and changed her lifestyle, they were treating the case "as a missing person where foul play is suspected."

Three months later, on April 22, RCMP issued yet another press release. This time they alerted the public to the disappearance of 21-year-old Maggie Burke. At 172 centimetres (5 feet 7 inches), and weighing 55 kilograms (120 pounds), Maggie was long and lean. With brown eyes and hair to match, she looks as though she could have been quite a beauty, but her eyes appear sad and withdrawn, almost troubled. Again, the police treated the disappearance as a suspected case of foul play. Again the announcement came after the grisly Camrose-area discovery of the body of another sex-trade worker—Charlene

Gauld. Charlene was only 20 and trying desperately to kick the drug addiction that kept her on the streets. Was there no end to the carnage? No end to the disappearances?

Sadly, Maggie's name was not the last that RCMP would draw attention to. On October 21, 2005, yet another press conference showed a photo of a dark-eyed, dark-haired beauty, her smile masking the pain 33-year-old Delores Brower must have felt. She was desperate to get out of the business, according to news coverage of her disappearance. JoAnn McCartney, a retired vice cop who was operating the diversion program for the city's Prostitution Action and Awareness Foundation, shared her memories of Delores with the *Edmonton Sun* on October 21. She recalled that the woman was a "tiny person," depressed with her life and longing for a new start. "Hopelessness is a huge thing on the street. People just feel there is no hope for them. She expressed that she didn't know if there was any point in hoping, or if there was any way there could be help for her," McCartney is quoted as saying in the news article.

The last time anyone had seen Delores was in the wee morning hours of May 13, 2004. It was about 5:40 AM when Project KARE members spotted the woman trying to catch a ride west on 118 Avenue. Although her family hadn't heard from her since earlier that month, a formal report of her disappearance wasn't made until June 2005. As with many other families, Delores' kin waited with anticipation, hoping week after week that she'd call, until they could wait no longer. She usually checked in from time to time. It had been too long since they'd last heard from her, and they were more than a little concerned.

Between the announcement of the missing Maggie Burke and the new press release of Delores Brower, RCMP had learned of the discovery of yet another murdered prostitute. Thirty-three-year-old Ellie May Meyer's body was found, dumped in a field in Strathcona County, just east of Highway 21 and north of Township Road 534. A farmer, planning to work through the night, made the grisly find on May 6, 2005. His plans quickly changed once he called police and they descended on his farm.

And then nothing—or at least nothing that made it into print. Although there may have been other missing women, RCMP weren't revealing anything haphazardly. They were, however, busy examining evidence and keeping their eyes on certain "people of interest." In a year's time, one of those individuals was no longer a person of interest. He was facing a murder charge, but not before another sex-trade worker was found murdered.

On May 7, 2006, the body of 36-year-old Theresa Merrie Innes was discovered stuffed into a hockey bag in a Fort Saskatchewan home. Her frantic family hadn't heard from the woman since the same time the previous year. The last time anyone remembered seeing Theresa was on September 5, 2005. Her family, no longer willing to wait for her phone call, reported her missing to the Edmonton Police Service on March 16, 2006. But by then, Theresa's brother, Mike, had been combing inner-city streets, conducting his own hunt for his sister for quite some time.

Various media outlets released two photos of Theresa. The much earlier photo shows a fresh-faced, 22-year-old young woman who looked like the last person you'd ever suspect would get involved in drugs and, subsequently, prostitution, to fund her habit. Friends described her as a hard-working, fun-loving woman who focused on whatever task she put her hand to and who was dedicated to her family and sons. Although she was known to work in bars from time to time, she didn't usually drink anything stronger than coffee. She did, however, struggle with an addiction to crack cocaine—a battle that she alternately won and lost. The last time Mike had seen his sister he had to stand firm against her drug addiction and asked her to leave his home. That was in August 2004. The next time he saw her was on May 11, 2006, when he identified her remains.

RCMP discovered Theresa's body after acting on a tip they'd received. She had been killed some time between her last sighting in September 2005 and May 7, 2006, when her body was found, but police hadn't pinpointed the time of death. Officials believed Theresa was murdered in High Level and that her body was later transported to Fort Saskatchewan. Compared with other similar discoveries, things were a bit different in Theresa's case. This time RCMP had a suspect, and on May 9, two days after her body was found, a 38-year-old High Level man named Thomas George Svekla was charged with Theresa's second-degree murder and with indecently interfering with human remains. Edmonton-area prostitutes and those involved in trying to help them get off the streets breathed a collective sigh of relief. Although no one was under the impression that Svekla was responsible for all the cases of missing and murdered women, the thought that at least one predator may have been apprehended had everyone feeling progress was being made.

That optimism soured, slightly, when *Edmonton Sun* reporter Andrew Hanon penned a special report on May 11, 2006, outlining how in late 2004 Svekla had sat before him in the newsroom asking him to help clear his name as a "person of interest" in the Rachel Quinney case. Hanon reported that Svekla had explained how he'd travelled with another prostitute to the area where Rachel's body had been discovered. He said the two had planned to do drugs, but that the prostitute got scared and ran from his vehicle. When Svekla set off to chase her, the pair stumbled over the deceased Rachel. Embarrassed that disclosing his findings to the police would mean he'd have to fess up to the reasons why he was there in the first place, he waited a couple of days, until he eventually "did the right thing" and called police. Now, Svekla claimed, he was being considered "a person of interest." After he dumped his concerns in Hanon's lap, apparently expecting him to do something about his circumstances, he left the *Sun*'s newspaper office, and Hanon didn't see nor hear from him again until the announcement of his arrest. Could it be that the man who once sat in Hanon's office was a multiple murderer?

Anyone who's ever traversed through the judicial system, whether it is for a divorce, adoption, civil proceeding or whatever, knows that to ensure success for your case, everything has to be in order. For the RCMP and members of Project KARE, any "person of interest" has to be investigated thoroughly, and something more than circumstantial evidence collected before they make an arrest. Without due diligence, it's quite possible a killer could go free. So it was in the investigation surrounding Rachel Quinney. Their suspicions about Svekla, even after his arrest in the Theresa Innes case, weren't enough to lay a second charge of murder—at least not yet. Law enforcement officials still had a lot of work to build a case.

A few days after Svekla's arrest, the body of another sex-trade worker was found in a rural area near Sherwood Park. Thirty-seven-year-old Bonnie Lynn Jack (a.k.a. Bonnie Lynn Loyie) was a sex-trade worker who operated in Edmonton and Vancouver. Because she travelled frequently between the two locations, and because in many cases prostitutes are trafficked between communities, a missing person's report hadn't been filed on her. Bonnie Lynn wasn't known to Project KARE, and the last time her family reported speaking with her was two months before her body was discovered.

As a spring thaw melts yet another white winter blanket, folks with loved ones partaking of a high-risk lifestyle, sex-trade workers and those involved in helping individuals out of that lifestyle collectively hold their breath, hoping against hope no other women will be found to have fallen victim to a predator or predators. But no one is fooling themselves. Somewhere out there someone knows more than they're letting on about this long line of misery. Someone may know what happened to Delores and Corrie and Maggie, and the many other missing women the public has yet to hear about.

In the meantime, court proceedings in the trial of Thomas Svekla on two murder charges began in February 2007. He maintained his innocence, saying it was merely coincidence that led him to the bodies of two murdered prostitutes. The RCMP and other Project KARE workers continue in their tireless efforts at putting an end to the carnage.

Chapter Five

The Land of Hungry Ghosts

I was there, once. Years ago. I think it was 1995. My family and I decided to stroll through Gastown on a summer holiday to BC's Lower Mainland. Avid art-lovers all of us, even my youngest at the time, only eight, was mesmerized by the many galleries and stores highlighting local talent. We wanted to take pictures of Gastown's famous steam clock, pick up chocolate creams at Water Street's Rodger's Chocolates, grab a snack here, check out a tourist trap there, and before you knew it, we'd strayed, ever so slightly.

On the street corner, a yellow cabbie parked, the driver leaning out his side window, blowing plumbs of cigarette smoke and staring ahead as if he was waiting for the light to turn green while the passenger in his back seat finalized a deal. It was all so apparent that even I, an all-things-drug-related virgin, knew what was going on. In a frantic gesture that was more comedic than protective, I ushered my kids away, like a mother duck with her ducklings, around the two men standing on the nearby sidewalk. We were obviously no threat as they didn't even try to camouflage their exchange, passing a mini-baggie of white stuff into the cab and accepting a few bills from the backseat occupant.

Surely this kind of thing doesn't go on in the middle of a tourist hub, I wondered? A few blocks farther along, with the remaining light of day all but extinguished, we quickened our steps in an effort to make our way back to that clock. We'd parked somewhere around there, or so we thought, and we were almost certain we were wandering in the right direction. Just a few steps in front of us a man, with dreadlocks so long they nearly swept the sidewalk behind him, popped out of a building and hurried ahead of us, only to slip into another a few doors down. The air was scented with something I couldn't quite put my finger on, and everywhere we looked, lights were flashing, and the folks gathered along the sidewalk all seemed to know each other. Maybe my unease was because I was a small-town-sort-of girl, I reasoned. It wasn't until years later that I learned the significance of our little stroll that night. Unbeknownst to me, I'd ushered my youngsters into Vancouver's Lower Eastside.

Known by the locals as "Low Track," the dozen or so blocks along Hastings Street just seconds away from the tourist-alluring Gastown is the poorest skid row in the entire country. Its centre, Main and Hastings, is commonly referred to as "Pain and Wastings" by the people who know this wasteland. With a location not far from the waterfront, drugs flow in and out of Vancouver like the tide, bringing with them rival suppliers frequently warring over who will feed the endless stream of addicts. Some statistics estimate that as many as 10,000 junkies live in the area. And one in four residents test positive for HIV or AIDS.

Today, Low Track has deteriorated far beyond the skid row I unintentionally toured 12 years ago. My son, now well into his 20s, lives on the waterfront about eight blocks away. He told me the homeless, the hookers, the disabled poor, the convicts, the addicts in various stages of withdrawal and the sheer depths of desolation he experienced in his one tour of the area in search of a particular business brought to mind the Buddhist idea of "hungry ghosts"—individuals who dwell in a realm of constant craving and addiction. Like the dark alleys of Batman's Gotham City, the historic buildings of Low Track stretch long and deep, imprisoning its inhabitants—or so it must have seemed to Marnie Frey. ∾

Born in Campbell River, BC, in 1973, Marnie practically lived outdoors. News reports profiling the missing woman uniformly portray her as kind-hearted, willing to give the shirt off her back and possessing a deep love for animals. As a youngster who dreamed of becoming a veterinarian, Marnie spent a great deal of her time near the family's chicken coop, keeping an eye on the flock of about 30 birds, playing with her bunnies or sitting quietly reading in one of her makeshift forts. Bubbly, attractive—effervescent almost—Marnie stood out among her peers as having that something extra we all aspire to. It was these qualities that formed the core of Marnie's person and kept her in constant contact with her family even after a cursory exposure to drugs quickly enveloped her in its grasp.

Unfortunately, as for many young women ensnared in the deceitful web of addiction, Marnie found herself living and working in the Lower Eastside, becoming one of the more than 80 percent of Low Track prostitutes migrating there from outside Vancouver. For most of these women, prostitution is the only way they know to support an increasingly expensive habit—one that renders them incapable of doing jobs requiring a clear mind. Even though she struggled with her addictions, Marnie never forgot her family. The last time they heard from her was on her birthday. She'd called home and talked to her stepmother, who said she'd be sending a care package Marnie's way. Marnie promised to call home when she received it. She never called. That was in August 1997. She was officially reported missing on September 4, 1998, but she was far from the first street worker to mysteriously disappear from Low Track.

That dubious distinction, according to the latest list of 65 missing Vancouver Eastside women, goes to Lillian O'Dare. She was last seen in September 1978. Since then, one, then another, name has been added. But there wasn't much of a "list" until Marnie went missing in 1997. That's when the Vancouver Police officially established a nine-member task force to look into the disappearances. By then, there were 20 names on that infamous list. By then, women's advocates and area residents had long since been calling for a concerted effort into investigating the disappearances. And by then, rumblings of a serial killer, even among the ranks of the police themselves, were getting a little louder.

The problem is, learning the whereabouts of an allegedly missing prostitute is sometimes difficult. Streetwalkers are a transient group, often moving from one community to another and at times even trafficked by their pimps to other locations. Law enforcement is often leery to admit that these women are missing. But those who lived on Low Track knew that the women they'd named as missing hadn't just moved on. They had left too abruptly. Many of them vanished, leaving behind their meagre, but valued, personal belongings. Some had made plans for the following day and never showed up. Those left behind on Low Track, along with the families of the missing women, like those of Marnie Frey, were convinced something was wrong.

Thirty-two-year-old Brenda Wolfe knew how to take care of herself. She was tough, often hired by Lower Eastside prostitutes for protection when she wasn't at her job as a waitress and bouncer at a local pub called the Balmoral. But she had a soft side, too, and was remembered by one bar patron in a news article as being "gentle like a kitten." Although she was tough and wasn't known to be a street worker, the last anyone had ever seen of her was in February 1999.

A month later, in March, 35-year-old Georgina Faith Papin, depressed that a child welfare hearing hadn't gone as she'd hoped, spent the last night she was seen downtown with a couple of friends. Also battling drug addiction, Georgina had managed to stay clean for periods of time in an effort to be the mother she dreamed of being to her seven children. They were her life, and she maintained contact with them as frequently as she was able, calling on birthdays and special holidays. A member of the Enoch Cree First Nation west of Edmonton, Georgina felt it important to instill an understanding of her heritage to her children. In a *Canadian Press* news article profiling the missing woman, Georgina's oldest child, Kristina Bateman, recalls how her mother once crafted a traditional dress, moccasins and beads for her and braided her hair for a powwow, where Kristina received the traditional name, Snowbird. Creating these and other cultural items was something Georgina was good at, and she dreamed of someday opening a store. Her dreams, like that of so many of the other missing women, were shattered prematurely.

Andrea Joesbury was just 23 when she was last seen. After failing to show up for the methadone treatments she'd been undergoing in an effort to get clean and to win back custody of her baby daughter, Andrea's own doctors reported her missing. That was in June 2001. Blonde, bright-eyed and sporting a beautiful wide smile, Andrea found herself living in the Abaddon that is Vancouver's Eastside when she followed a boyfriend from

Victoria to Vancouver. Several years her senior, the boyfriend turned out to have other plans for the young love-struck teen, and instead of being that hero she envisioned, he introduced her to drugs. From there the step into prostitution was a small one—it's often the only way to survive for these women. But Andrea, on her way out of that lifestyle, was robbed of hope for a new life, a hope she was earnestly working towards.

At the age of 29, Sereena Abotsway was also on her way to beginning a new life. She, too, struggled with addiction and supported her habit through prostitution. But as a woman born with fetal alcohol syndrome, her journey to health was doubly difficult. Even in the midst of living on the streets, and despite dealing with her own demons, Sereena's thoughts were for her Eastside sisters. She marched in rallies advocating a more dedicated approach to the investigations surrounding Low Track disappearances. She attended a Main Street church and through her actions lived the Gospel in a way many without her difficulties never do.

Cheryl Bear Barnetson, a church worker interviewed by *Canadian Press*, recalled a time when Sereena helped a man no one else wanted to approach. "I don't know if he was high or drunk or what, but…you could just kind of smell that he had gone to the bathroom in his pants," Barnetson was quoted as saying. "He was a mess. She just jumped in right away with no hesitation and just started helping him." It was that kind of selflessness Sereena was known for.

At just 27, Mona Wilson had already fought long with a heroine addiction that kept her shackled to the streets. A survivor of childhood abuse, Mona had some good years. From age 8 to 13 she lived with a foster family who, by all accounts, treated her as one of their own. She had a hand in the daily chores, but she was also part of the fun, too. That she remained attached to the family since her move to another foster home was evident in her regular calls to them. Typically, her conversations must have been somewhat superficial since her foster family wasn't aware of her drug addiction or how she supported her habit. The hell Mona was living, however, would rapidly become all too clear.

What the watching world soon learned is that these six women (Marnie Frey, Brenda Wolfe, Georgina Papin, Andrea Joesbury, Sereena Abotsway, Mona Wilson) all shared the same fate. They all went missing and remained that way until their remains were discovered on the grounds of Robert William Pickton's Port Coquitlam pig farm. It is these six women, along with 20 others, that he stood charged of allegedly murdering by the time his first trial kicked into motion in early 2007.

Mona's foster brother, Greg Garley, took in the first few weeks of the court proceedings. His thoughts were chronicled in the *Prince George Free Press* in April of that year.

"It's Jeffrey Dahmer and Clifford Olson all rolled into one," he said to reporters. "It makes them look like amateurs. My sister's head was found sliced in two. [The perpetrator] didn't just decapitate them, he sliced their heads in half…desecrated their bodies…reduced them down to a butchered carcass."

Long before dozens of anthropologists and an additional troupe of investigators descended on the Pickton farm, and long before the pig farmer sat in a courtroom listening to witnesses for the prosecution list their evidence against him, there had been rumours on the streets. Whenever a girl went missing in what many referred to as the "War Zone," others would talk. Some suggested a serial killer was at work. The thought wasn't well accepted initially, but the question posed by former detective inspector Kim Rossmo in the October 2001 issue of *Vancouver Magazine* was, "If it's a bunch of different people, why are we not finding bodies?"

A 1999 *Calgary Sun* article posited the fear that a "sex-slave slaughter involving the ships in the harbour" was making the rounds among sex-trade workers. The fear appeared to have had at least some grounding after one woman was reportedly lured to a ship with the promise of a limitless supply of heroin, only to be held there against her will and passed around from one man to another. It wasn't an isolated story among prostitutes working the Eastside. And street workers often theorized that some of their missing sisters may have been lured onto a ship with the promise of drugs, but instead of breaking free were murdered and dumped in the sea. One statistic points out that roughly 95 percent of the country's illegal heroin supply makes its way into Canada via the shores of Vancouver, so the story seemed even to investigators to be a plausible one.

There was also some talk about a farm—and about not going down there. But it wasn't until the RCMP secured a search warrant and raided Pickton's home looking for illegal weapons and discovered personal items belonging to some of the missing women that the property was cordoned off and digging began. What followed was the equivalent of a mass exhumation that uncovered, at last published account, 27 DNA profiles. Here are the faces behind the science. *(Many personal comments and remembrances about these women were taken from the Vancouver Eastside Missing Women Internet message board.)*

Aside from a few messages on the Internet message board dedicated to Vancouver's missing and murdered women, not much is known about Diana Melnick's life before her arrival in Low Track. Born in 1975, she was just 20 when she was reported missing in December 1995. "She was a kind and warm person," Ken Phillip writes in May 2005. A 2002 message written by Emily Norris recalls Diana as a typical youngster who loved horses and excitedly awaited the next school dance. "I hope someone finds her and brings her home," she wrote. "It is not a nice place to be lost."

Tanya Holyk wanted to get straight. A little more than a year before she vanished, on October 29, 1996, Tanya called her sister, Cathy Hall, and begged to come home. Cathy was all for Tanya moving in, but she needed a few weeks to complete work on her house. Tanya, though trying desperately to stay clean for her newborn son, took the response as rejection and hung up. It was the last Cathy heard from her sister.

Twenty-five-year-old Cara Ellis first hit the streets of Calgary to escape the memories of being raped and to support her drug habit, but when a friend was killed by a john, she moved on to Vancouver. Struggling with her addictions, Cara tried several times to detox and make a better life for herself. But as her sister-in-law, Lori-Ann Ellis, said in a news report, "Unfortunately she was in a position where the drugs were speaking for her. She would basically prostitute herself in order to be able to get the next fix and get the next fix in order to be able to prostitute herself. So, it was a really vicious circle." Cara was last seen in January 1997.

Andrea Borhaven's life could be paralleled to the song lyric "lookin' for love in all the wrong places." Born in 1972, Andrea was just a toddler when her parents separated. She spent the majority of her childhood living alternately with her mother, father or other relatives, desperate to feel loved and yet unable to accept it when it was given to her. Andrea was diagnosed with attention deficit hyperactivity disorder, and Andrea's mother, Sharon Hall, tried to get her the help she needed, but by 13 she was already getting into trouble at school and experimenting with drugs. At the age of 16, Andrea was living independently, and it wasn't long after that she was living on the streets of the Lower Eastside. Just before Andrea disappeared, Sharon received Andrea's personal items via Greyhound. She was coming home and was determined to clean up. And then nothing. Andrea was last seen in 1997.

Loving yes, but it was her independent streak that lured Sherry Irving from a loving family into the throes of a rough crowd where drugs were plentiful and experimentation the norm. But her family never gave up on her, and Sherry faithfully kept in touch. Her brother, Chris Irving, an elected band councillor in the Aboriginal community of Mount Currie, reported his sister missing after she stopped calling home. She was last seen in April 1997.

Troubles at home and a succession of unsuccessful foster home placements propelled Helen Hallmark into experimenting with drugs by the time she was in her early teens. Although her addictions eventually led her into life on the streets to support her habit, she was compassionate and caring to the point of even protecting a friend from walking the same path. "I was going through a very confusing, tough time in my life. It would have been very easy for me to turn to drugs and prostitution," a woman going only by the name of Anita writes in 2002. "When I met her I did not do drugs and she and her friends took me under their wing and basically sheltered me, preventing me from entering the lifestyle." Helen would have turned 31 just days after she went missing on June 15, 1997.

When 47-year-old Cynthia Feliks went missing in December 1997, family members weren't immediately worried.

She'd disappeared at other times but always came home for a little familial TLC to "get healthy." This time, though, Cynthia didn't resurface, and her Low Track friends were getting worried. Despite struggling with her own personal demons, she was always known to have a sparkle to her smile and an ear for anyone in need. "Cindy…was so full of life and we miss her very much," her stepmother Marilyn Kraft wrote.

Whatever possessed 39-year-old Kerry Koski to first try heroin with no previous history of drug use remains a mystery to those who knew and loved her. For the most part, the single mother adored her three daughters, lived a regular, middle-class life and had friends and family who loved her. Her choice in men, however, left something to be desired. Her last boyfriend was the person to introduce her to heroin, and within three months of trying the drug, Kerry was sucked out of her otherwise stable life, landing hard in Low Track. "Kerry was a beautiful person and I hope that is how she is remembered," her childhood friend Dawn Bourque said in a *Canadian Press* article. "It's how I remember her." Her family last saw her at a Christmas dinner in 1997. She was last seen on the street on January 7, 1998.

Inga Hall was born in Germany and moved to Ontario as a youngster, but by the age of 14 she had left home and was taking care of herself on the street. In between stints as a street worker, Inga maintained a couple of long-term relationships. She was married once and gave birth to a daughter. A second little girl was born years later in a second relationship, but Inga's addiction kept her on the streets of Low Track working to fund her drug habit, and in time, that daughter moved in with her paternal grandparents. Inga was last seen on March 3, 1998.

Probably the most well known of the missing Eastside women is Sarah de Vries. Born in 1969, Sarah was adopted at the age of 11 months by Jan and Pat de Vries. The youngest of four children, Sarah was doted on and well loved. But she had challenges from birth, and as an adult she was thought to have the intellect of an 11-year-old. When she was 14 she ran away from her adoptive home in search of the excitement she thought only the city could offer her. Whatever the lure, eventually she, too, found herself gripped by drugs—a death grip that kept her on the street and away from the two children she bore and loved dearly. She was an avid writer and artist and used every scrap of paper she could find to express her feelings. "To others it was just a drawing, but to me it was my laugh, smile, thoughts, feelings, ideas, pain (lots of pain)," one entry read. These poems and journal entries are part of a book entitled *Missing Sarah*, penned by Sarah's older sister Maggie. Sarah was last seen on April 12, 1998.

Angela Jardine disappeared in November 1998 at the age of 28. Angela was mentally challenged and estimated to have the intellect of an 11-year-old—a "little girl trapped into a woman's body" as her mother once was quoted as saying. In many ways Angela used a well-equipped imagination to fit into the world around her. A john wasn't someone who paid her for sex.

Instead, she'd introduce them to her fellow street workers as a family member or long-lost friend. She was a chameleon of sorts; if she didn't like the way she felt in her own skin one day, she'd just adopt another persona. On the day she disappeared, Angela was introducing herself as the police chief's daughter. For her, life was all about fitting in and looking for love and acceptance.

Well read and politically aware was how Elaine Allan, who once worked at a Downtown Eastside drop-in centre called the Women's Information and Safe House (WISH), described Jacqueline McDonell in a *Canadian Press* article. At just 23, Jacqueline was a loving mother to a daughter born to her when she was just 18. Everything she did was focused on her baby girl, until she fell in love with a recovering drug addict who introduced her to the drug scene. Shortly afterwards, she tried to clean up, but when that didn't happen, she lost custody of her daughter to her mother. She may have been a regular at the drop-in, but her time on Low Track was remarkably short-lived. The last confirmed sighting of her was on January 16, 1999.

Childhood friends as well as those who knew Jennifer Furminger on the street would describe the 28-year-old as shy but playful, funny and possessing incredible talent as an artist. Jennifer went missing in December 1999. Her remains were discovered on the Port Coquitlam pig farm owned by Robert Pickton and positively identified in February 2003.

Wendy Crawford was 43 and a mother of two when she disappeared in December 1999. Her sister, Susie Kinshella, remembers Wendy as a hardworking, loving mother, sister, aunt and friend. Susie explained in a letter submitted to *Canadian Press* that a desperate attempt to provide for her family led Wendy to the Eastside.

In an online message board entry, Tiffany Louise Drew was remembered as "the sweet little girl with the long blond hair and the face of an angel and the heart of a tiger" by a woman who babysat her as a youngster. Sweet, feisty and possessing of a magnetic personality was also the way Elaine Allan of WISH remembered her in a *Canadian Press* article. When Tiffany didn't come home one day, her roommate and Allan reported Tiffany missing to police. Months later, Tiffany's roommate received word that Tiffany was in a recovery program and didn't want any contact with her former life. It was years later that a newspaper reporter called Tiffany's roommate to say she was listed among the dead discovered on the Pickton pig farm. Tiffany was 25 years old when she was last seen in March 2000.

For Kathleen McKenzie, her 42-year-old sister Debra Lynn Jones is much loved and dearly missed. "She sang like Janis Joplin, and she played guitar, piano, music, dreamed of going to Nashville one day," Kathleen writes in 2004. "She was a mother, a niece, a loving sister and a daughter to a mother. She was much more than drugs...she had no reason to be butchered like she was." Debra vanished in December 2000.

Photographer Lincoln Clarke was quoted by *Canadian Press* as saying Patricia Johnson was "really bubbly and an absolute delight to be around…she had this stunning aura about her that was noticeable…she kind of looked like a little ray of sunshine was following her." At 16, Patricia was living alone and supporting herself. A boyfriend came along shortly thereafter, followed by a baby by the time she was 17. In the end, she had two children, Eric and Autumn. She had each of their names tattooed in a rose along the left side of her back—it was her way of keeping them near her after a series of small but significant events separated the young mother from her boyfriend and children, and she found herself living in Low Track. "She was not proud of what she was doing," her mother-in-law, Laura Tompkins, was quoted as saying at a Vancouver peace forum. "But she was a person with a lot of dignity and inner strength." She was last seen in March 2001. She was 26.

Heather Chinnock was described by those who knew her as "happy-go-lucky," but in the grips of drug and alcohol addiction, even her upbeat personality couldn't keep her off the streets. Adamant that she was not a prostitute, Heather preferred to shoplift to fund her habits. Still, as a last resort, the 31-year-old must have turned to the trade at least a couple of times, since she was arrested twice on related charges. She was last seen on April 1, 2001.

By the time 34-year-old Dianne Rock disappeared in October 2001 she was a mother of five and was holding down a succession of stable jobs. For a time she worked as a health-care aide in a nursing home in Ontario and later as a support worker for mentally challenged adults in Abbotsford. But somewhere in between these two positions, which showed Dianne's loving character to its fullest, the mother found herself in need of work and took the only job available—an exotic dancer. Those closest to her think this is where she first tried cocaine as a means to gather the courage she needed to get up on stage. After an overdose in 1992, she and her family moved to BC in an effort to make a fresh start. It worked for a time. Dianne loved her job and was attending college classes in Surrey. But by 2000 her marriage ended, and it's thought that she slowly started to rely on her old friend cocaine again. By April 2001 she'd taken a leave of absence but never returned to work as expected and was last seen that October.

There was nothing unstable about Heather Bottomley's home life. To look at the missing person's photo of the diminutive 25-year-old, it's hard to imagine anything was ever awry. With dimpled cheeks, eyes that draw you in and a smile that almost screams mischief, the petite mother of two looks a lot like the girl next door. But she wasn't. As with many Eastside stories, hooking up with the wrong man landed her with a drug addiction and, as it turned out, a life sentence in Low Track. She was last seen in 2001.

~

As of this writing, Pickton is charged with allegedly murdering these 26 women. Another charge of murder had to be dropped because, though DNA was identified, investigators couldn't match it to a name, and a CBC news report stated a judge had ruled that "Pickton could not be tried for killing an unidentified victim." According to an April 5, 2007, report penned by Ethan Baron of Can West News Service, "Pickton does not contest the fact that remains of the six women he's [currently] on trial for allegedly killing were found at his farm, but he denies killing them."

Not to be forgotten are the remaining names on the list of 65 women currently confirmed as missing since 1978, and the names considered for addition. Whether Pickton will eventually face additional murder charges for any of these women remains to be seen. In the meantime, these women, who were mothers, sisters, daughters and friends, were loved. And they are still missing.

Rebecca Funo, last seen in June 1983; Sherry Rail, November 1983; Marlene Abigosis, January 1984; Sheryl Donahue, May 1985; Laura Mah, August 1985; Elaine Allenback, March 1986; Teressa Williams, July 1988; Ingred Soet, August 1989; Elaine Dumba, 1991; Nancy Clark, August 1991; Elsie Sebastian, June 1992; Kathleen Wattley, June 1992; Sherry Baker, January 1993; Gloria Fedyshyn, February 1993; Teresa Triff, April 1993; Leigh Miner, December 1993; Angela Arseneault, August 1994; Catherine Gonzalez, March 1995; Catherine Knight, April 1995; Dorothy Spence, August 1995; Frances Young, April 1996; Olivia William, December 1996; Marie Laliberte, January 1997; Stephanie Lane, January 1997; Jacqueline Murdock, January 1997; Sharon

Ward, February 1997; Richard "Kellie" Little, April 1997; Janet Henry, June 1997; Ruby Hardy, July 1997; Cindy Beck, September 1997; Tania Petersen, February 1998; Sheila Egan, July 1998; Julie Young, October 1998; Marcella Creison, December 1998; Michelle Gurney, December 1998; Dawn Crey, November 2000; Sharon Abraham, December 2000; and Yvonne Boen, March 2001.

Chapter Six
Follow Your Daughter Home

Long before The Guess Who recorded the smash hit "Follow Your Daughter Home," fathers with daughters, and big brothers with sisters, have traditionally looked out for the womenfolk of their family. Sadly, they've had to. Pegged as little more than chattel, a woman's worth was usually measured by the men in her life. It's little wonder, then, why women have been victimized throughout history and still are to this day. Predators consider them easy targets, the "weaker of the species," and of no more value than what pleasure can be derived from their use. In reality, perhaps our most devastating downfall is our nurturing and trusting nature. Women like to think the best of people; I know I do. Sometimes, though, that's gotten women into trouble. In some of the cases that follow, a trusting nature could be blamed for leading a woman into dangerous places. In other cases, what led to her disappearance remains a complete mystery. ✎

LAS VEGAS BOUND

Imagine…

Pretty, pink and endearing from her first wail—a daughter named Jessica Edith Louise, born May 27, 1984. Mom is so pleased with her new warm bundle that the thrill is almost enough for her to forget the recent labour pains. Dad…well, he can't take his eyes off his little darling.

Before long the newborn has grown into a toddler, and then even bigger. She's playing in the sand and splashing against the big waves washing up along the beach, learning how to swim and hanging out with friends. Soon she's marching up to get her high school diploma, and then, in the blink of an eye, she's gone. A young adult now, she spreads her wings and learns to fly. Mom and Dad find it worrisome to let go. It's always hard to let go. And so much harder when the one you love doesn't return home.

Such was the scenario faced by Glendene Grant and Dwight Foster. Although the couple had separated before Jessie reached her first birthday, both maintained a strong bond with their daughter. During her formative years, Jessie lived in Kamloops with her mother. Glendene enrolled her daughter in swim lessons, Brownies, Guides, dance lessons and the church camp, and she saw Jessie through elementary, junior high and most of high school. When Jessie was very young, Glendene met Jim Hoflin, and the couple began a long relationship that despite their current struggles, remains strong to this day. Other children came along, and life at home was generally pretty good.

Early in Jessie's grade 11 year, she moved in with her father and stepmother in Calgary to finish high school. Dwight had always mourned the fact that he'd missed out on Jessie's youth, and the father and daughter used those years as time for bonding. In 2005 Jessie moved back to Kamloops. But after taking several trips to a few U.S. hotspots—Fort Lauderdale, New York City, Atlanta City—Jessie knew she wanted to move south. That May she chose to settle in Las Vegas. Her two worried parents might not have liked the idea of their darling daughter living anywhere with a reputation like "sin city," but what could they do? As any parent knows, putting up roadblocks accomplishes little more than a breakdown in communication. So everyone gritted their teeth, kissed and hugged Jessie goodbye and prayed for the best.

In November Jessie returned to Calgary and then Kamloops for an extended visit to both her parents' homes during the Christmas season, returning to Las Vegas on the 3:00 PM flight out of Kamloops on Christmas Day. Although it was the last time they were all together, Jessie frequently called her family members, sometimes daily. The last known contact anyone had with Jessie was when she spoke with her sister Crystal on March 28, 2006. Then nothing. No answer on her cell phone. No banking activity. No charges to her credit cards. Silence.

Jessie was officially reported missing by Glendene on April 9, 2006, after first calling Peter Todd, the individual Glendene had thought was Jessie's live-in boyfriend. During that phone call, Peter told Glendene that Jessie had moved out at the beginning of April, and he didn't know her whereabouts. The North Las Vegas Police Department and the RCMP were both called. Dwight also hired a Las Vegas private investigator. And in time, at least some answers came trickling in to the family, but they weren't necessarily answers they were prepared for.

It appeared that Peter Todd—the well-to-do Prince Charming Jessie had told her family about, the man who'd swept her off her feet and was to a large degree the impetus for her move to Las Vegas—was allegedly more foe than friend. The talk about town was that Peter Todd was actually a pimp who'd recently separated from his wife, a known prostitute. It's an accusation Peter vigorously denied. Furthermore, on questioning Peter, investigators learned that Jessie may have also fallen into that line of work, either willingly or through coercion. The news shocked the family.

"She's a good kid....We're talking about a girl who got 'A's on her report card. She never smoked cigarettes. She never did drugs," Glendene told *Global National*'s news reporters during one interview.

And if this wasn't enough of a shock, the news got worse. Peter's estranged wife had threatened Jessie several times, frightening her enough to keep her from answering the front door if she was home alone for fear that the "ex" was on the other side. It was a concern Jessie voiced many times and Peter later confirmed.

As shocking as this news was to Glendene and Dwight, regardless of what their daughter did for a living, she was still their daughter. She was still that little girl who loved to play in the water and build castles in the sand, and no one had the right to harm her. They had to act quickly if they were going to find her.

Along with hiring their own private investigator, Jessie's family began creating and distributing missing persons posters, contacting media and garnering publicity for their plight. They knew that the more they kept Jessie's face in the public, the better chances they had of finding her. They developed a website (www.jessiefoster.ca) with family pictures, a chronicled account of Jessie's early years and later disappearance, copies of every news article written about her and information on Jessie's vital statistics. And in the year following her disappearance, Glendene and Dwight made several trips to the city that never sleeps. Since Jessie's been gone, every waking moment has been dedicated to finding her. That's the way it has to be. Until they know otherwise, Jessie's family continues to believe that she's still alive.

"I have since the beginning felt that she has been a victim of human trafficking," Glendene said in a *Kamloops This Week* article dated March 16, 2007. "Therefore, not only do I believe she is alive, but I believe that she is being held against her will somewhere."

The suggestion that Jessie may have become a victim of human trafficking isn't the result of a panicked parent, nor is it the imagining born of television and movie dramas. Human trafficking is a sad reality, even here in the Western world we believe to be so civilized and beyond its earlier dark history of slavery. Statistics released in June 2006 by the U.S. Department of State reports that "between 600,000 and 800,000 people are trafficked across transnational borders, or from one country to another each year. When intra-country or 'within country' estimates are included, the figure rises into the millions."

Women and children are often abducted from one country and transported to another, enslaved by their captors and forced into sexual and other forms of exploitation. Sometimes these victims are simply moved from one corner of the country to another. Either way, if Jessie became a victim of human trafficking, she could be anywhere in the U.S. or in some far-off land overseas. The North Las Vegas Police must have agreed at least to some degree with Glendene's assessment that abduction by human traffickers could be a possibility, because Jessie's case has since been moved to the ATLAS (Anti-Trafficking League Against Slavery) task force and the vice squad in the Metro Las Vegas Police Department (LVPD).

As the Metro LVPD grudgingly added yet another case to their ever-burgeoning workload, arguing repeatedly that in Jessie's case they have yet to determine any evidence of criminal wrongdoing, Glendene continues to do her part. She makes sure everyone has heard of Jessie and can identify her if they see her, by maintaining a public presence for her daughter and garnering as much media attention as possible, especially in the U.S., because that's where Jessie was last known to be seen. Just say the name "Laci Petersen" and an image of the sparkly-eyed brunette with the bobbed haircut and brilliant smile immediately comes to mind. That's what Glendene wants for Jessica. She wants people to experience that immediate recognition so that if they see her anywhere, they'll know her story and will call the authorities. To that end, Glendene has appeared on several American talk shows, the most recent being *The Montel Williams Show* in New York City, where she told Jessie's story.

Like any mother in her situation, every once in a while Glendene gets caught up in "what ifs," such as when she remembers driving Jessie to the Kamloops airport the afternoon of Christmas Day, 2005. Glendene and Dwight likely wish they could have talked Jessie out of leaving. They probably also wonder if there was anything they could have done to prevent their daughter from getting caught up with a dangerous crowd. And they miss her so very much.

"Jessie is the second out of four sisters. They are very, very close, and this gap in their sisterhood is so huge it is unimaginable," Glendene said. "This is how it is with all of us. Just a small little girl like Jessie and she leaves a hole too huge to imagine when she is not there to fill it.

"Jessie was a tomboy when she was in elementary school and when she got to high school she blossomed into the most beautiful young woman. She is petite and always has her hair and makeup done. However, she can belch louder than a drunken sailor and can spit farther than any man I know. She has a wonderful sense of humour and always has a smile on her beautiful face."

But Jessie's family can't let themselves become distracted by memories and reminiscing. There are fundraisers to host, investigators to check with, media to inform, a website to update. Doing these things are the only ways that the family can survive this ongoing purgatory and hold on to that thin strand of hope that in time, they will find some kind of resolution. ∾

A FORKED TONGUE?

Parents are constantly reinforcing to their children the need to be wary of strangers. But they think that they should be able to trust those in authority implicitly—doctors, police, teachers, preachers. It was the case of the latter, or at least an affiliate with ties to a religious organization, that led to a heart-wrenching experience for an Ontario family living on Manitoulin Island.

To begin at the beginning, the events that eventually led to Heather Moggy's disappearance on June 22, 2002, started in the early 1990s. According to a document written by Colorado author Robert L. Peterson, who chronicled a considerable portion of the history of the Brethren Assemblies in North America, that's when three couples moved to the island's Manitowaning area. They were Christopher and Veronica Cawte, Alvin and Jackie Cook, and John and Kelly Tucsok and their families. The Cawtes ventured into the area first, in 1990, and began attending the already established Gospel Hall in Gore Bay where Christopher became an elder in 1994. That same year, the Cooks and Tucsoks moved to the region, and together, the three families founded the breakaway Clover Valley church.

An island just off the southern shores of Ontario in Lake Huron, Manitoulin stands apart from the rest of the country, connected only by the Highway 6 south bridge or, during the busy holiday season, by the Chi-Cheemaun ferry. The area prides itself on its natural beauty and rich Native heritage. Avid outdoors enthusiasts and artists of all mediums flock to the island for inspiration and rejuvenation. Perhaps it's the feeling of remoteness or the freethinking quality of the residents that attracts folks of all backgrounds to the area, but either way, the residents of Manitoulin Island generally accept people, and the establishment of a new Gospel Hall was as welcome as the next batch of tourists.

When the Cawtes, Cooks and Tucsoks initially pulled away from the Gore Bay church in September 1994, the fledgling congregation began meeting at the old Clover Valley Schoolhouse. After two years of worshipping there, the members renamed it the Clover Valley Gospel Hall. News stories in the *Manitoulin Expositor*, an e-newspaper covering the local scene, describe how the church, its methods and the messages preached there produced a magnetic-like allure to the area's young people. The image is fairly representative of the experience of Melvin and Linda Moggy's daughter Heather.

Although Heather was the sixth of eight children, Linda Moggy described her relationship with her daughter as close. Born on February 16, 1985, Heather shared her mother's birthday, and Linda felt her new bundle of joy was the best gift any mother could ask for. The blonde-haired, blue-eyed youngster grew into a beautiful young woman who, at 17, was as curious about the world around her as anyone else that age. Maybe even more so, given the fact she'd lived on the island her entire life, and trips to bigger centres were rare. Perhaps that's why she was so drawn to the meetings held at the Clover Valley Gospel Hall. Really, though, it didn't matter why she attended. It was church, right? At an age when some city youngsters are getting into drugs and the party life, the Moggys were likely thrilled that their daughter's teenage obsession was going to the local meeting hall to praise the Lord. No harm there…or so they thought.

It wasn't long before Linda started feeling a bit odd about the whole thing. The more Heather attended the church, the larger the gap Linda felt growing between her and her daughter—definitely not the kind of result indicative of Christian teaching as Linda understood it. Other parents were also growing concerned, especially parents of young women. Some reported feeling that their youth were being "conned" into joining what seemed more like a cult than a legitimate church. They felt that the young people in the community were being targeted because they were more easily swayed into believing the specific brand of doctrine preached by this church. And there was more.

Some parents expressed concerns that their daughters were being sought out and preyed upon by one elder in particular—John Tucsok. At first John seemed like a nice enough fellow. Married with four children, John home-schooled his youngsters and was thought to be an all-round handy kind of guy. But as time went on and John was often seen in the company of young ladies half his age, tongues started wagging. He was known to counsel some of these young girls in "private," and at a church picnic another young lady was seen to be "feeding him a sandwich, like they were a young married couple." Linda tried to advise her daughter against attending the church, but Heather continued to go, frequently picked up at the family's home by John. In time, discontent with John turned into allegations of improper conduct between him and some of these young girls. That's when John disappeared, leaving wife and children behind and apparently taking Heather with him.

Over the last few years the Moggys have actively sought information on their daughter's whereabouts. At one point they discovered that Heather and John shared a post office box in Brantford, and in the fall of 2003 Heather called home, saying she was planning to move from Calgary to Saskatchewan. Other rumoured sightings have filtered through to the Moggys, who still live in Manitoulin, but that telephone call was the last time Linda heard her daughter's voice.

For the Moggy family, their beloved daughter is missing. Heather is also listed as a missing person on the Ontario Provincial Police's Resolve website. But by all outward appearances, Heather left of her own accord and is not thought to be a victim of foul play. True, she was likely heavily influenced by John Tucsok and his unique interpretation of the Bible, but it's difficult, if not impossible, to prove the heavy hand of coercion in this or any other case of someone taking off with an allegedly duplicitous leader. Still, Linda wishes her daughter would at least call home and let the family know how she's doing.

At the time of her disappearance, Heather was just 17 years old. Although Heather is simply listed as a missing person, John is wanted by the Ontario police on several offences. ∾

THE GIRL NEXT DOOR

Kimberly Anne McAndrew was the kind of person who enjoyed every challenge life had to throw at her. At 19, the young woman had already spent a year at Dalhousie University and was making money for the fall term by working a summer job at a Canadian Tire store on Quinpool Road in Halifax, Nova Scotia, just a few minutes walk from the apartment she and her two sisters shared.

On a particularly quiet August 12, 1989, Kimberly's work supervisor decided to reward his hard-working employee by allowing her to clock out early. Kimberly punched her time card at 4:21 PM. It was a sunny Saturday, and she had plans for the evening. Life was good. The day before, she had arranged for her sister to pick her up from work at the end of her shift, which would have been about 5:00 PM. But because she had gotten off early, Kimberly decided to set out on foot, tackling a few errands on the way.

According to the Halifax Regional Police, Kimberly was last seen at the Gardenia Flower Shop in Penhorn Mall in Dartmouth. An employee at the shop remembered the cheerful, happy-go-lucky young woman with a flashy smile and wavy blonde hair purchasing a balloon and a rose. She then walked out the shop door, and that was the last anyone saw of her.

Meanwhile, Kimberly's boyfriend, her sister and her sister's boyfriend, unaware she'd gotten off work early, were on their way to Canadian Tire to pick her up. When they discovered she'd left early, and that none of them had spotted her as they drove there, they immediately raised the alarm. She most certainly should have been walking along the very route they'd just travelled.

As with any missing persons case, police and family members examine every possible angle, beginning with the possibility that the allegedly missing person left of his or her own accord. But Kimberly, considered a well-adjusted, happy, level-headed young woman, didn't fit the profile of someone who would choose to disappear. No matter how deeply they probed into Kimberly's life, police saw absolutely no indication that she was distressed or upset about anything. As well, if leaving on purpose was even the remotest of possibilities, Kimberly certainly wouldn't have chosen that day to leave. She was scheduled to have her braces removed early the following week, and she was excited at the prospect. To all who knew her, it simply didn't seem feasible that she'd gone off for a few days without letting anyone know. It wasn't long before law enforcement personnel admitted they had to agree with Kimberly's loved ones. But if she hadn't left of her own accord, and because no accidents had been reported between Canadian Tire and Kimberly's home, there was only one other possible answer to her disappearance— she must have been taken against her will.

Immediately, police officers focused a great deal of attention on her case. People who knew Kimberly thought her to be a sweet girl with an upbeat personality, someone who got along with everyone, the real "girl next door." Her disappearance touched the hearts of the tight-knit community from the moment it was made public. It also sent a ripple of fear through the area. How could something like this happen, and in broad daylight?

Over the years, police have followed up on tips, conducted interviews and polygraph tests, and even checked out information sent in by psychics, but not so much as one of the jade green, flat-heeled, slip-on loafers she was wearing, or the balloon and flower she purchased that day, have ever turned up.

Tips continue to trickle in all these years later. Every report of a possible sighting brings with it hope and devastation to Kimberly's family—hope that maybe an answer has been uncovered, and devastation when the tip turns out to be a dead end.

Today, 18 years after she vanished, the case remains open. Her family still prays for a miracle that someone somewhere will find the courage to come forward with information. The Government of the Province of Nova Scotia has maintained a $50,000 reward for "information leading to the arrest and conviction of the person(s) responsible" for Kimberly's disappearance. It expires November 25, 2007. ∾

VANISHED

An evening drive meant as a way to unwind after a hard day's work ended in a mystery that today, 15 years later, remains unsolved.

The story begins around 11:30 on the hot night of August 28, 1992. Thirty-five-year-old Janice Howe arrived at her parents' home in the Winnipeg neighbourhood of Fort Garry after a gruelling workday. Looking for a way to shake off the tensions from her shift, Janice asked her father if she could borrow his car for an evening drive. It was her way of letting loose. Just roll down the window, head a few kilometres out of town and feel the warm evening air whip through your hair. There was a sense of freedom in that, an almost cleansing experience, and Janice was in need of a little stress relief.

Borrowing the family car was never a problem. Janice's father always made sure the car had a full tank of gas, oil change up to date, fluid levels filled—Mr. Howe was meticulous when it came to his car. The last he and his wife saw of their spry, energetic, bubbly blonde daughter was when they waved good-bye as she pulled out of the family's driveway.

That's when the mystery begins.

No one—not her parents, friends or investigators—was able to determine where she went from her parents' home nor how her father's vehicle, a 1985 blue Olds Ciera, ended up 220 kilometres away, abandoned on Highway 1 and not far from the small city of Kenora, Ontario. In fact, investigators didn't know whether Janice drove herself, if someone else had driven the car or if perhaps at some point the car was stolen and Janice wasn't even a passenger at all.

There were other strange unknowns in the case as well. The car was discovered around 10:00 AM the day after Janice's disappearance, by Ontario Provincial Police (OPP) who were scouting the area for an injured deer. After examining the vehicle and locating the car's owner, they discovered that several things didn't add up. For example, Janice's father maintained immaculate records, jotting down an odometer reading every time he set out in his vehicle and when he returned. That way he could keep track of his vehicle's gas consumption. Although the car was found 220 kilometres away from the family's home, according to Mr. Howe's records, it had been driven a lot farther than that—550 kilometres, in fact. Where the car had been the other 300-plus kilometres is unknown. And while no blood was discovered in the car, investigators noted the rear floor mats were missing, as was a tarp, adding yet another dimension of concern for the missing woman's well-being.

At first, investigators thought Janice may have for some reason become disoriented by her surroundings and wandered from the vehicle after parking it on the shoulder. With that in mind, the nearby bush was searched. An underwater team was dispatched to scour a nearby lake, thinking Janice may have wandered there and drowned, but no additional clues were uncovered.

Another, albeit far-fetched, scenario suggests Janice may have suffered an acute case of amnesia and never recovered. Should that be the case, police, along with OPP, circulated information on the missing woman, asking anyone who might have come in contact with someone fitting her general description living in and around eastern Manitoba or northwestern Ontario to call their nearest detachment.

Although police have considered that Janice may have met with foul play, to date, her body has never been discovered, and the case remains an active missing person's case.

From the night she vanished, neither Janice's bank accounts nor her credit cards have been used—it's the one piece of concrete evidence investigators do have. A DNA profile, along with dental records, is also on file for comparison should someone matching Janice's description come forward or should any unidentified, skeletal remains be discovered.

Chapter Seven

When Missing Becomes Murder

The first thought to occur to someone who's had a loved one go missing is for his or her safety. Are they all right? Are they cold or hungry? Are they being harmed or tormented in any way? And then there's the ultimate question that grips every heart with an unstoppable fear—will they come home safe?

Statistics show that to the great relief of family and friends, most missing persons do return home safely. But for the 4800 people who are still missing a year after their disappearance was first reported, hope for a happy reunion grows thin. By this point many families might still be praying for a miracle, and indeed such miracles have occurred. But at the very least, family and friends are hoping for some sort of closure. If their beloved is deceased, discovering the remains is one way to come to grips with the finality of their fate and begin the grieving and healing process.

For some of the cases that follow, a body was eventually discovered. In other stories, a missing person is officially declared "murdered" because of the evidence collected, even though a body has not been discovered. Either way, a family's worst nightmare is most definitely realized when missing becomes murder. ❧

IN YOUR OWN BACKYARD

How they met or what kept Viola and Jim Leahy together from the very beginning of their courtship in 1950 appears a bit of a mystery. Hard-working and dedicated to the farm that had been in the Leahy clan for four generations of Leahy farmers, Jim took his position as caretaker to the family homestead very seriously. He also wasn't averse to supplementing his many farm chores by offering his heavy excavation equipment services to neighbouring farmers. It was early to bed and early to rise for the rather staid Jim Leahy.

Before her marriage at the age of 40, Viola worked as a registered nursing assistant—a position she held for a time even after her marriage in 1951. She enjoyed socializing, and although she wasn't a drinker, she loved to go to the local tavern or hotel to take in the music and have a partner swing her around the dance floor. Viola had personality and sparkle and, since opposites seem to attract, perhaps it was this very quality that first drew Jim to her side.

In time, though, Viola left her nursing position, and as she neared her mid-60s was experiencing frequent memory lapses, partly resulting from arteriosclerosis—a thickening of the arteries that reduces blood flow. Her discomfort at being alone at home for prolonged periods and having a husband who was always away initiated a number of disagreements, one that resulted in Viola leaving the farm for a time and starting separation proceedings. Some sort of peace pact was reached, however, and Viola returned to the farm, though the couple's subsequent living arrangements were now more like roommates than husband and wife. Both had their own bedrooms and their own bank accounts, and they pretty much kept to themselves.

Viola maintained the home, made meals and did the laundry throughout the week. But on the weekends, her brother Jack Leeson and his wife Zetta would drive the interaction-starved Viola to the Peterborough home of her girlfriend, Emgard Woodzack. Emgard, 25 years Viola's junior, in some ways may have represented the daughter she never had, and the two women hit it off immediately, ever since first meeting as out-patients at a Peterborough health clinic. Week after week, Viola headed down to Emgard's on a Friday night and returned home Monday evening. The two women, along with a couple of male friends, were weekend regulars at a couple of Peterborough nightspots, taking in whatever band was playing and dancing the night away. It was a routine Viola lived for, and it helped her cope with the loneliness the remainder of the week held for her.

Friday, September 17, 1976, was like many other Friday nights before then. Jack and Zetta fetched Viola and her suitcase from the 100-acre farm that represented little more than desolation to her and trekked her down to the big city. As usual, Viola was bubbling over with excitement, and as usual, the weekend whizzed by all too quickly. Though she loved them dearly, Viola was never too thrilled to see Jack and Zetta on Mondays, ready to take her back home for the week. That following Monday, Viola was feeling under the weather and had booked a doctor's appointment for that evening. The ever diligent Jack and Zetta brought Viola to her doctor's appointment and then back to the farm. Viola usually phoned Zetta several times a day, so Zetta and Jack weren't too concerned—they knew they were only a phone call away.

But when Viola didn't check in later that night, and when Tuesday came around with still no phone call, the couple started to get worried. On Wednesday morning, after calling Viola several times, they still couldn't get in touch with her, so Zetta and Jack decided to call around in person. What they found, and what they didn't find, equally disturbed them. Viola's suitcase remained where they had left it Monday night. The couch had been moved into an irregular position, a couple of items were overturned, and although neither Viola nor Jim smoked, the ashtray was full of butts. What there was no sign of, however, was either Viola or Jim.

A quick call was made to Jim's brother, who lived on the neighbouring property, and the mystery of Jim's whereabouts was solved. Several years previous, Jim had been in a farming accident, and the previous Sunday he'd been scheduled for some follow-up surgery in Toronto. He hadn't told Viola of his plans, because he'd be away for a few days and didn't want her filling the house with her friends.

So with one mystery solved, Viola's whereabouts was still unknown. When by Saturday she hadn't turned up, the police were contacted—but an investigation was not immediately undertaken. Because the family was concerned, the police set about a cursory review of the case, but there were enough speculation about Viola feeling discontent with her life on the farm that police thought it wasn't completely unlikely she'd chosen to leave. When Jim returned from Toronto, he noticed most of her clothes were still there, so he pooh-poohed everyone's concern, reasoning she'd return soon enough. And when the public were asked for their assistance via two Peterborough radio stations, a couple of inaccurate tips surfaced: one was that Viola had been seen about 12 days after that Monday, in the company of a fellow at a Peterborough hotel, dancing. It was later discovered that the caller mistook the date and the sighting actually took place the weekend of September 17.

It took a bit longer to confirm that the other tip was a sham. A postmaster, on hearing the public appeal for information on the woman, recalled a change of address notice he'd received for that same name, requesting mail be rerouted from the Rural Route #4 Lakefield address of the Leahy farm to the Sudbury Post Office. Police contacted the Sudbury location, asking the postmaster to inform them if the woman ever came by to pick up her mail. She hadn't. And when several months' worth of social security cheques sat uncashed, and it was clear Viola hadn't made any bank transactions since her disappearance, concerns among law enforcement were beginning to point to something far more serious than a disgruntled woman breaking away from the humdrum of her daily life. By then, police were talking murder.

In January 1977, Ontario Provincial Police Constable Gary Katz took over the investigation and was soon joined by Detective Inspector Atholl Smith of the Criminal Investigation Branch. From their initial inspection of the change of address card, it was determined that the writing wasn't Viola's and the document was forged. Their first course of action, then, was to determine who had planted this misleading piece of evidence. Handwriting samples were taken from everyone initially interviewed, and each, in turn, were eliminated.

However, there was one person whose writing sample police hadn't compared. That individual was 19-year-old Ralph Leahy, the son of Jim's brother, Emmet. At the time of Viola's disappearance, Ralph was living with his father and occasionally helped out his Uncle Jim with the farm chores. Now he was living with his girlfriend, Barbara Hartwick, in Edmonton, Alberta. Eventually, a writing sample was obtained from the teen's old high school, and it matched the writing on the change of address card. But why would Ralph forge the document? Had he murdered his aunt, and if so, why? Because nothing appeared to be missing from the farmhouse, robbery didn't seem to be a motive. The whole scenario just didn't make any sense.

With absolutely no proof whatsoever of Ralph's involvement with his missing aunt, the only evidence police could move on was the forged document. In April, Smith and Katz travelled to Edmonton to interview Ralph, who first denied committing the forgery, then said some man paid him $50 to do it. It wasn't enough for a charge of murder, but it was enough for a charge of forgery. Although his dad posted his bail, Ralph returned to jail for a three-month sentence at the Quinte Regional Detention Centre in Napanee following his June trial. Now that police had him behind bars, they had to move quickly to get him to confess to murdering his aunt. Detective Inspector Bill Perrin had replaced Smith on the case, and just before Ralph was scheduled for release, Perrin sent Constable Bill Campbell of the Intelligence Branch to pose as a fellow inmate. The ruse worked, and before long Campbell had Ralph confessing not only to the murder, but also to a long list of other crimes, most of which he hadn't committed, in an effort to get in on Campbell's "illegal money-making schemes" once they were both released. Campbell was expecting to be out any day on bail, and Ralph was released August 9.

The pair met up the next day, and then at another meeting a few days later, Campbell brought along Constable Terry Hall, posing as his brother and partner in crime. Ralph continued to brag about his previous crimes, and just to prove his boast that he'd killed his aunt, he volunteered to take Campbell and Hall to the site on the farm where he'd buried her body. Under the cover of darkness, Ralph and the two constables made their way to the farm and started digging. And digging. And after several fruitless hours, the body, which Ralph estimated hadn't been buried more than a foot underground, still hadn't been recovered. Frustrated, the trio left the scene.

For a short time, police attempted to play out the scenario in the hope that Ralph would eventually lead the undercover agents to the body. But Perrin decided to pull the plug on the investigation, arrested Ralph and brought in his girlfriend for questioning. It only took a little probing by Perrin to have the frightened young woman, now eight months pregnant, tell police everything she knew. She explained how Ralph told her the entire story shortly after he'd shot his aunt three times and buried her in her own farmyard. It didn't take much from that point for Ralph to fess up to the murder to police and lead them to the body. It took several days of digging and the eventual use of some heavy-duty equipment before the body of Viola Leahy was finally uncovered on August 30. She'd been buried almost a year.

When asked why he had murdered his aunt, Ralph simply said he didn't like her. His only regret was he'd been caught and would be spending far more time in jail than he thought the old lady was worth. He was found guilty, but a subsequent appeal lowered Ralph's original 16-year sentence to 10. ✺

Snatched from School

Elizabeth Marie Bain was the embodiment of the perfect daughter. She had a radiant glow about her that emanated a gentle, sweet spirit and only added to her outer charm. The brown-eyed, dark-haired beauty was barely 157 centimetres (5 feet 2 inches) tall and weighed 49 kilograms (108 pounds), and although anyone who caught a glimpse of her would surely agree she was gorgeous, it certainly wasn't something she appeared to be aware of. Elizabeth was more concerned with being a good friend, a good daughter, a good student. An interest in people is what motivated the 22-year-old to study psychology at the University of Toronto's Scarborough campus. Between her family obligations, her studies, her work at Metro Social Services, extra-curricular activities and her many friends, Elizabeth's life was as full and invigorating as any young woman's life should be. But all that was about to change.

At around 4:00 PM on Tuesday, June 19, 1990, Elizabeth grabbed her car keys, hugged her mother Julita goodbye and said she'd be home in time for supper. She had a few errands to run, which included a stop at the library and a quick check of the tennis schedule. She also had a class that night at 7:00 PM, so her timeline was a tight one. Elizabeth was used to the fast pace, though, and never complained. Her mother smiled as her only daughter rushed out the family home, the door slamming behind her.

The Scarborough campus isn't that far from the Bain's family home, and before long Elizabeth was mulling through the book stacks and taking care of her returns. Witnesses later remember seeing the young woman at the library as late as 5:30 PM, and she was seen sitting with a man at a picnic table near the tennis courts at around 6:00 PM.

But she didn't make it home in time for dinner. Nor did she make it to her 7:00 PM class. She never made it home at all. Julita and husband Ricardo spent a sleepless night of worry before they could wait no longer and reported Elizabeth missing at 6:45 the following morning. She'd only been gone a little over 12 hours, but the couple knew their daughter. For Elizabeth, missing dinner and not coming home for the night without so much as a telephone call wasn't a commonplace occurrence. The Bains didn't remember her ever being so thoughtless. Something was definitely wrong.

Although police were cautious at becoming involved—arguing it wasn't out of the realm of possibility for a young woman to have any number of reasons for an unannounced overnight excursion—they agreed to look into the situation. Just a couple of days later, the Bains' worst fears were all but confirmed when Elizabeth's 1981 two-door Toyota Tercel was discovered about one kilometre away from the family's home and near an auto body shop. A large bloodstain in the car's back seat immediately propelled the case from the status of a missing person to that of a possible homicide. The Metro Toronto Police homicide unit immediately took over responsibility for the case. The car was towed to the Centre for Forensic Sciences, and Elizabeth's parents each submitted a blood sample to determine if the blood from the car was a DNA match to their daughter. It was.

Over the next several days, Metro Police, family and volunteers gathered numerous times to conduct intense ground searches throughout the university campus, around Elizabeth's family home and near the site where her car was discovered. While concrete evidence eluded police, circumstances led them to focus on one possible suspect in Elizabeth's abduction and possible murder, and that was none other than Elizabeth's boyfriend Rob Baltovich. Very early on into the investigation, the stability of Elizabeth and Rob's relationship was brought into question, and Rob, for the most part, took a spectator's role when it came to volunteer searches and the like. Although he was questioned at length by Metro Police, he refused to take a lie detector test. However, the 25-year-old had earlier stated he'd seen Elizabeth's car parked on Old Kingston Road at about 6:45 on the night of her disappearance, and that it was gone by the time he passed by again around 9:20 PM.

As days turned into weeks and months, Elizabeth's father and others continued to search for anything they could find to shed some light on what happened to the young woman. In the meantime, police were continuing to build a case against Rob. Elizabeth's diaries were uncovered, and in them she'd written about concerns over her and Rob's relationship on several occasions. Some of Elizabeth's friends reported to police that she and Rob were having "problems," and police noticed that several pages in one of Elizabeth's diaries had been torn out. Reports of Rob's obsessive nature and extreme jealousy, accurate or not, were surfacing from numerous sources, and before too long he was charged with her murder.

Although the prosecution didn't have a body, they had what appeared to be at least part of a crime scene—the large bloodstain in the back seat of Elizabeth's car. Experts testified at trial that the back seat was conducive to having a large, bulky and bloodied object dragged across it. On April 1, 1992, Rob Baltovich was found guilty of Elizabeth's murder, and although the family had yet to put their daughter to rest in the honourable way they had hoped to, they could at least accept partial closure in knowing that the person responsible for Elizabeth's demise would be duly punished.

But the story doesn't end there. Although a considerable circumstantial case had been built against the one-time boyfriend, a good portion of which was developed from comments or suggestions Rob himself made during various interviews, he did win the right to appeal his case. On March 31, 2000, he was released from prison pending that appeal. On December 2, 2004, the Ontario Court of Appeal further set aside Rob's murder conviction, ordering a new trial. The formal announcement of that new trial was made the following year, on July 15, and was set to begin in early 2007. Pending the outcome of that trial, Rob was again presumed innocent of the crime he'd been charged of and vehemently denied committing all along. And his lawyers had what they thought was a plausible explanation for Elizabeth's disappearance. During Rob's earlier arrest and throughout his first trial, defence lawyers continued to introduce the possibility that Elizabeth was actually another one of Scarborough-rapist and convicted murderer Paul Bernardo's victims. Bernardo wasn't charged with the succession of rapes in the Scarborough area until 1993, and in 1995 he was convicted of the deaths of Leslie Mahaffy, Kristen French and Tammy Homolka. At least one witness placed Elizabeth in the company of a blond man some time before her abduction, and Bernardo had attended the University of Toronto Scarborough campus the same time Elizabeth had. It was a consideration Rob's defence attorneys would continue exploring.

Another possibility for Elizabeth's disappearance was raised by a woman who testified in court, saying her brother-in-law Patrick Mahoney lived near the campus and jogged along the same trails as Elizabeth. She went on to explain that after 20 years of experiencing alleged sexual abuse from Mahoney, she'd finally garnered the courage to have him formally charged. Mahoney had since fled to Ireland.

Will any of these theories provide the solid answers the Bain family is looking for? Is it possible Bernardo or some other predator is responsible for Elizabeth's death? Or is Rob Baltovich guilty, after all? Only time will tell. In the meantime, in the case of Elizabeth Bain, missing rapidly became murder. But for her family, murder or not, their daughter is still not home. ∾

PHOTO SHOOT GONE BAD

At the age of 23, Natel King was tall, beautiful and feisty as all get out. Anxious to raise the money needed for her college tuition, the psychology student (a.k.a. Taylor Sumers) confided in her mother Jackie something that most mothers wouldn't be anxious to hear—her darling daughter had opted for a short-term career in the world of adult entertainment. Jackie later told NBC reporters that her daughter had been warned by the family that "this is an area that is very dangerous and she may not have the control she thinks she has." But as with most young people that age, Natel was convinced she could take good care of herself. She also took her own unique precautions, such as refusing to do scenes with men. And the money she could earn would certainly take care of her financial worries.

By early 2004 Natel had already worked in at least one erotic film, but she made it known that her preference was print. That February, the Mississauga resident landed a photo shoot scheduled for February 29, in the Philadelphia suburb of Conshohocken, Pennsylvania. Natel had been approached for the job, along with another adult film star and a friend of Natel's named Autumn Rayne. Autumn had turned down the job, thinking the photographer involved, Anthony Frederick, was "too creepy." But the $900 US Natel could earn would go a long way for a Canadian college kid, and she just couldn't turn down that kind of cash. So she packed up her 1992 red Saturn and headed south for a few days.

By the time she geared up for the Philadelphia photo shoot, Natel had seen enough in her short career that the photographer's props probably didn't come as a surprise, but some time during her session she felt uneasy and decided to call Curtis Shears, her roommate back in Mississauga. He later told *Toronto Sun* reporters that Natel admitted to him that she, too, thought the photographer was weird and that she was worried. When Curtis asked her if she was "worried about not getting paid or getting killed...she said, 'I don't know. Both.'"

That phone call, coupled with Natel not calling her family, something she did regularly when away on business, was likely a huge impetus in her family's decision to call police and report her missing. Soon after, Natel's car was discovered abandoned in the Conshohocken neighbourhood where she was scheduled to meet with her photographer, raising concerns over Natel's several day absence even more. Still, a routine inquiry with photography assistant Jennifer Mitkus led police to believe Natel left the shoot safe and sound, heading out to find something to eat after being paid her $900.

As the days wore on, concern for Natel's welfare turned into anxiety, unlike anything her parents had ever experienced before. On March 23, their worst fears were realized when

Natel's partially decomposed body was discovered, apparently tossed over a nine-metre drop to the Schuylkill River below. Had there been a rise in the river level, Natel's body could have very well been swept away along the scenic waterway and dumped into the Delaware River farther south. As luck would have it, that didn't happen. Natel's family would find some consolation in knowing what became of their daughter, and the discovery of her body gave them hope that the perpetrator of the crime would be quickly identified and apprehended.

Even with the decomposition that had taken place, it was easy to see the information provided to police by the photography studio was erroneous. Natel couldn't have walked away from the photo shoot, because she had been bound and gagged in the fetish gear she had worn for the photos, and she was wrapped in the same backdrop material that the photographer had used that day. She was stabbed repeatedly in the chest and neck, and her defensive wounds indicated that she fought hard to save her life. Evidence of bondage items, equipment stained with what was later determined to be her blood and a graphic poem about death were all recovered from the studio, and 47-year-old Anthony Frederick was charged with Natel's murder.

Frederick later pleaded guilty to her murder, saying he hadn't had the money to pay her, and when he informed her of this, she came at him first, with his knife. Although authorities didn't believe self-defence was a motive for a crime—even if that had been the case, clearly overkill was involved—they accepted his plea in exchange for a reduction of the charge to third-degree murder and for testifying against his assistant Jennifer Mitkus. She stands charged with "abuse of a corpse, hindering apprehension, conspiracy to abuse a corpse and conspiracy to lie to authorities."

Anthony Frederick could spend anywhere from 23 to 51 years in prison for his crime. He was denied an appeal in December 2006. ∾

THE TWILIGHT ZONE

Located on the shores of Lake Huron, the area that now makes up Ontario's Municipality of Kincardine has been a hub of activity ever since freighters and steamships first used the waterway back in the mid-1800s. Not only was the area well suited for settlement—and towns like Kincardine sprouted and thrived—but its sandy beaches and the almost innate love of festivities by its residents have blended to make the region a visitor's paradise. With the town's annual music festival, Madisons Haunted Inn, Sunday singalongs, nightly serenades, weekly flea markets, parks, museums and so on, there's never a shortage of things to do in Kincardine.

On July 3, 1988, 25-year-old Lois Marie Hanna was enjoying one of the many activities her hometown had to offer. That night, the former beauty queen and fashion design student attended the "Celebrate In '88" reunion dance in the nearby

Village of Lucknow. Eager to reconnect with old friends and let her hair down a bit, Lois mulled through the crowds, caught up with what was going on in the lives of many of her schoolmates and enjoyed the music. But fairly early on that evening Lois complained of being tired, and at 11:30 PM she bid her brother David and their friends goodnight and headed back to her red brick bungalow on Nelson Street in Kincardine. It was a Sunday night, after all, and Lois was on opening shift the next day at MacG's, the Kincardine clothing store where she worked. Feeling the way she did, she knew a good night's sleep was necessary for her to meet her Monday obligations.

Weary though she was, Lois thought a cup of tea was in order, so when she arrived home she turned on the kettle on her way to her bedroom. Perhaps she lingered a while to consider what she'd wear the next day as she put the night's party garb into her closet. Then it was on with her favourite peachy-pink nightgown and back to the kettle, now sounding loudly in the background. Cup of tea in hand, Lois sat on her favourite living room chair and turned on the television. She knew she could only indulge in the welcomed quiet for a short while if she was to get to work on time the next morning.

She never made it in on time. In fact, she never made it in at all.

Her absence wasn't discovered until 11:00 AM on Monday, when the store manager Debbie MacGregor arrived at work, only to find the doors locked. Once she completed the store's opening routine, she phoned her absent employee. The entire scenario was highly out of character for the well-mannered, level-headed and responsible Lois. Concerned when there was no answer at Lois' home, MacGregor dispatched another store employee to check on Lois.

What greeted the woman when she went to the house was eerie. All the doors to Lois' home were locked, which seemed strange, since her 1987 Grand Am was parked in the driveway, and it appeared that she must be home. The clerk knocked on the front door gently at first, then with considerable force. No answer. Touring around the home, the woman noticed that the bathroom window was open. Determined to enter the home, Lois' co-worker squeezed through the small opening and was finally inside.

It was clear that Lois had made it home from the party in one piece the night before. The outfit she'd worn had been returned to her closet; her purse and all its contents were in the china cabinet where she always kept it; the television was on; and aside from a half cup of tea sitting on the counter, not a thing was out of place. But Lois was nowhere in sight.

The police and Lois' family were contacted. Lois' mother and brothers were immediately concerned, as were Lois' co-workers. The whole scenario didn't make sense. Police asked family members to carefully make their way through Lois' home to determine what, if anything, might be missing. Not much, it appeared. And except for Lois and her favourite peachy-pink nightie and matching housecoat, everything else was accounted for. It didn't appear that Lois had faced any kind of confrontation, since there was no sign of forced entry and nothing was out of place. It was like a story out of Alfred Hitchcock's *Twilight Zone*—a story that to date hasn't produced any kind of conclusion.

Even under the suspicious circumstances that appeared to surround Lois' apparent disappearance, law enforcement personnel proceeded with caution. After all, Lois was an adult, and perhaps she had chosen to leave for a while. Perhaps there was a secret lover in her life who'd swept her away for a few days. But by that Thursday, the Ontario Provincial Police had been called in, and the investigation moved forward with more force.

Over the following years, between police and Lois' family, an estimated 1000-square-kilometre area around Kincardine was searched. Hundreds of tips were followed up, and even a psychic was consulted, who insisted that Lois' body was dumped in the middle of the night by a stranger passing a cornfield or an area with brush. Every time someone reports seeing buzzards circling overhead, the Hanna family still cringes, wondering.

Living in such close proximity to Lake Huron resulted in a few crushing blows for Lois' family as well. In little more than a two-week period spanning late April and early May 1990, the lake would give up no less than eight bodies. With each discovery the Hanna family, and others with missing loved ones, would experience agony and anguish words alone are helpless to describe. None of those remains were that of Lois Hanna. Worn and weary, her loved ones would once again pick up and continue on—there was little else they could do. Eventually Lois' home had to be sold, her hard-earned possessions packed up and put into storage, leaving her loved ones torn with the thoughts that they'd given up on Lois ever coming home, and what if—what if she was alive somewhere?

Details of the investigation are closely guarded because police believe Lois was a victim of foul play, and they continue to investigate the case. Her picture and particulars are on the Ontario Provincial Police's website, and although the case was officially upgraded to a murder case in 1998, she also remains listed as a missing person. In 1999, blood evidence was lifted from Lois' home and analyzed, and police at the time believed they had a solid suspect. Since then no further official information has been released.

Police suspect that either someone was waiting for Lois or that she was followed home from the reunion. In 1998, another 10-year reunion was held, and police set up an information booth hoping to collect a few more tips. In 2008 yet another reunion is scheduled. Hopefully it won't also signify the 20-year anniversary of a still-unsolved mystery. ∾

NO REASON TO RUN

The summer of 1988 spelled change for Lisa Maas. The 22-year-old had recently separated from her common-law husband and was looking forward to starting over. She was also five months pregnant—a situation she was thrilled about, and all who knew Lisa reported she was eagerly awaiting the arrival of her first baby.

On July 17, Lisa attended a house party in Woodford, Ontario. As the night drew on, it was made apparent that the host's brother didn't have a ride home. Since Lisa hadn't been drinking, she agreed to drive him to his home in nearby Annan. That was the last anyone saw of her.

"It's always in your mind, every day," her mother June Reimer told *Court TV* in an on-camera interview. "You keep hoping and for a long time every time we'd go out we'd be looking for Lisa. You go on with your life because you have to, but it's always there."

For June and her husband Ken, Lisa's pregnancy made it all the less likely she would just skip town. Newly separated, Lisa had returned to her parents' home to live and was looking forward to their help in raising her child when the time came.

When Lisa's 1975 olive-green Plymouth was discovered by farmer a few days after her disappearance, concern for Lisa's welfare deepened. It was stuck in the mud down an Owen Sound country road referred to by some folks as the local "lovers' lane."

Not far from the car, police also found her driver's licence and her mud-covered camera. It was beginning to look as though Lisa may have come in harm's way, and a massive search of the vicinity ensued.

And that's where the case goes cold.

The disappearance of Lois Hanna less than two weeks earlier in roughly the same corner of Ontario set the region's residents and police on edge. Although there has never been an official suggestion linking the two cases, there are similarities. Both women were about the same age, both were petite, both were well-liked and family-centred individuals, and both were as happy with their lives as most of us will ever be. The two women also disappeared in close proximity to one another, both geographically and in terms of time. And both families are still waiting for answers.

In 1990, the Reimers posted a $50,000 reward for information leading to the whereabouts of their daughter. They also went big when it came to getting the word out to the public, plastering the information on several billboards. Although tips have trickled in through the years, more often than not they've resulted in a lot of effort being exerted without any payoff in terms of producing a solid lead.

As recently as 2004, another ground search was launched by OPP officers, this time just south of Owen Sound on a rock ledge. Prompted by what appeared to be a legitimate tip, trained climbers and cadaver dogs combed the area looking for even the smallest sign of Lisa. Sadly for Lisa's parents and family, this, like so many other tips, has proven fruitless. Now well into their retirement, June and Ken Reimer still hope for an answer to what happened to their beloved daughter; it would be the best gift anyone could give them. ∾

VALENTINE VICTIM

Twenty-four-year-old Roxanne Fernando of Winnipeg should have been on the top of the world. At least, that's what she planned as she readied herself for a night out with her boyfriend, 19-year-old Nathanael Mark Plourde. It was Thursday, February 15, 2007, and since the couple had missed out on their Valentine Day celebrations the day previous, they were planning a night out to make up for it. Roxanne was thrilled. She'd chosen three gifts for her sweetheart, and before leaving for her outing, her mother helped her wrap them. That time together would be the last memory Roxanne's mother would have of her beloved daughter.

At about 6:30 PM, hair appropriately coiffed and makeup in place, Roxanne headed out for dinner. Perhaps the couple would have a steak at The Keg or dig into a bowl of steaming pasta at the Spaghetti Factory; Roxanne wasn't sure. She was quite certain, though, that this would be a night to remember.

And remember it her family most certainly would, but not for the happy reasons Roxanne may have contemplated.

When she didn't come home that night, and concerned for the young woman's well-being, Roxanne's family reported her missing. A brief mention of her made it into that Friday's *Winnipeg Sun*. Height: 5 feet 8 inches [173 centimetres]. Weight: 130 pounds [59 kilograms]. Hair: medium brown, long and straight. Clothing: jeans, brown jacket, pink runners. Being so close to deadline, the paper was lucky to manage these sparse details. The same information was again circulated in the next day's news.

But after one, then another day went by, and Roxanne remained on Winnipeg's missing persons list, her family grew increasingly worried. Roxanne, who'd moved to Winnipeg from the Philippines just three years earlier, was a responsible, hard-working individual who held down two jobs. She shared a home with her sister—family was very important to Roxanne. Something terrible must have happened.

The days stretched on, feeling like an eternity to the Fernando family. Mercifully they wouldn't have to wait long to learn of their daughter's sad fate. On February 26, less than two weeks after she'd gone missing, the Fernandos and Winnipeg's Filipino community that had gathered in support of the missing girl's family would learn the shocking truth—missing, in this case, had become murder. Periodic warm days had melted away enough of Winnipeg's typically deep dump of winter snow, and Roxanne's lifeless body was discovered poking through what remained in a ditch in the city's northwest. An autopsy conducted a few days later indicated that Roxanne had died from being struck several times with a blunt object. The autopsy also suggested she'd died the night of her romantic rendezvous, and that she was newly pregnant.

Although nothing can make up for the loss of a life, the speedy recovery of Roxanne's body can at least afford the family the small comfort of being able to provide their loved one with a proper burial. The family can also take comfort in knowing that the three individuals thought responsible for her demise were captured and charged with her alleged, premeditated, first-degree murder. Those charged include her boyfriend, Nathanael Mark Plourde, 19-year-old Jose Manuel Toruno and a 17-year-old boy who could not be named. ∾

THE KILLER NEXT DOOR

A typical summer day in Markham, Ontario, was remarkably tame for 25-year-old Alicia Ross. The spry and energetic young woman had experienced a taste for the outdoors at a fairly early age and was already well travelled, having adventured from the deserts of the Negev and Judea in Israel to the Amazon River and many points in-between. Nevertheless, Pomona Mills Park was like a little piece of heaven amid a bustling metropolis, and walking along its pathways was the perfect way to unwind after a busy day at work.

And so it was that on the evening of August 17, 2005, Alicia and her mother, Sharon Fortis, took the family's dogs for a leisurely stroll, all the while discussing the great summer they were all having. Alicia had a new boyfriend, was expecting a promotion at work and was planning a trip to Costa Rica's lush rainforests. "This is your summer. You deserve it," Sharon remembered telling her.

Later that night, Alicia's new boyfriend, Sean Hine, stopped by, and the two went out for a bit, played a few games of pool and burned some CDs. Then he dropped her off back at the family home, where Alicia lived in a downstairs apartment. Sharon bid her daughter goodnight around 11 PM, and Sean left to go home around midnight. Alicia then readied herself for bed. Her mom and stepfather had long since retired, and to all outward appearances, the night seemed like any other.

But the next day, when Alicia didn't show up to work, Sean called her home and cell phone. When he couldn't get in touch with her, he called 911 and reported her missing—an action that would later put him under immediate suspicion since it seemed an extreme measure to take for someone who was simply late for work. Sean then called Alicia's parents, who immediately rushed home from work only to find, in stunned amazement, that police were already at the house and searching for the missing woman. What they discovered fairly quickly was that while nothing had been disturbed in Alicia's apartment, with her purse, keys, car and everything where it should be, it appeared she'd been in some type of struggle outside in the family's backyard. Her shoes were found splayed across the grass, along with a drinking glass and a cigarette, and the back gate was left ajar. It appeared as though she'd been abducted.

Family and friends were questioned right away, as was the last person known to have seen the young woman—Sean Hine. Although never officially referred to as a suspect, in less than a week after Alicia's disappearance, Sean had been called a person of interest in the case by the police and reported as such in the news. Sean, distraught over the apparent abduction of his newfound love and overwhelmed by what he felt was intense interrogation by police, pulled away from the media spotlight and Alicia's family.

Meanwhile, extensive searches were underway, led by scores of police and padded significantly by a steady stream of volunteers. News outlets continued to run stories on the missing woman and her grieving loved ones, and Alicia's mother, initially reluctant to expose her entire family to what was fast becoming a media circus, broke her silence and pleaded for anyone who knew something to come forward. In this one act of faith, which propelled countless stories to follow about the beautiful young woman with a smile that could melt your heart and a family praying for her safe return, Alicia became a daughter to the entire population of the Greater Toronto Area.

Police continued to forge ahead with their investigation. As there were few leads, and they were unable to uncover any additional clues, police began suspecting Alicia had become a victim of foul play. The Ontario Provincial Police behavioural science unit had suggested she was likely abducted by someone she knew, but that theory only puzzled family and friends more. Alicia was well liked by everyone. Who would want to hurt her, and why?

By this point, well-meaning but ill-informed psychics had started contacting the family with visions of where they believed Alicia was. Anxious to try anything, various family members travelled to Barrie, to Parry Sound, to Woodbridge, and other locations, following up on these suggestions, only to meet with disappointment. But there were helpful developments as well. Cards and letters of support began pouring into the family home. It was a good thing, too. The family would soon need all the support it could get.

On the one-month anniversary of Alicia's disappearance, Sharon was once again in front of the media as television cameras filmed and newspaper reporters penned emotion-packed stories. "I need her back," Sharon said in a *Toronto Star* article. That plea, along with the thought that the wrong man could be charged with Alicia's murder, combined with what lawyer David Hobson said were feelings of "great remorse," propelled 31-year-old Daniel Sylvester to step forward and surrender to police on September 20. He then led police to two locations northeast of the city, one was near the Sylvester family's Coboconk cottage, where human remains were recovered and later confirmed to be those of Alicia Ross.

The announcement sent shockwaves throughout the community, but perhaps nowhere more so than with the Ross and Fortis families themselves. Just days after Alicia's disappearance, the family's 70-year-old neighbour told reporters how unbelievable it was to think you weren't even safe in your own backyard anymore. Now it turned out that that same neighbour was none other than Olga Sylvester, and it was her own son who'd allegedly committed the crime.

When asked, friends of the Sylvester family almost uniformly expressed shock at the revelation. Although Daniel was thought to be a loner, lived with his mother and didn't have a job to speak of, he was remembered as a "great big, good-looking kid" who loved reading and came from a well-adjusted and happy home. What could have motivated the man to allegedly commit murder won't be known until his second-degree murder trial is heard sometime in 2007.

Sharon, Alicia's stepdad Julius and her seven siblings gathered on October 7 to bid their precious loved one a last farewell. More than 1500 people listened as Sharon recalled how the beautiful, blonde-haired, blue-eyed, chubby-cheeked cherub who she and her first husband, Marvin, adopted as a newborn grew into an "adorable and good baby, a precocious toddler, a blossoming pre-teen, and a terrible, terrible teenager" and later into a "spirited, yet warm and understanding young woman."

And as the funeral procession made its way to Pardes Shalom Cemetery, police officers displayed a unified show of support as they staffed each intersection along the way, holding back traffic and saluting. "Alicia Ross Laid to Rest" the next day's newspaper headlines would read, and a chapter would close in a very tragic saga that gripped an entire city and will continue until the question "why" is finally answered.

Chapter Eight

Missing by Misadventure

In scouring a variety of missing persons databases on the Internet, be it the internationally renowned Doe Network or RCMP and other law enforcement websites, a significant number of individuals who have disappeared are thought to be victims of accidents. Unfortunately, without some sort of confirmation that a loved one met with an accidental death—the discovery of the deceased's body, for example—family and friends are left hanging in the worst kind of limbo. Imaginations run into overdrive. Thanks in part to the wonders of television, film and many a great mystery book, the mind probes all kinds of possibilities. What if our Johnny staged an accident to make it appear that he'd died, but in reality he had gone off to start a new life? What if he made it through the accident and was struggling, somewhere, to make it home safely? What if the accident left him with amnesia, and he was wandering around homeless and not knowing who he is? What if a loved one committed suicide? For some, these questions and countless others are never answered. For others, confirmation of their loved-one's demise offers a mixed blessing—the chance to grieve, but with the reality that there is no hope of a happier ending. ∽

THE GOOD SON

Twenty-two-year-old Joe Gledhill Jr. had just moved back home with his parents, Marilyn and Joe Sr., in their family home in Chester, Nova Scotia, after working in Newfoundland and New Brunswick for two years. Joe Jr. was the only child of a very close-knit and loving family, and so his decision to move closer to home thrilled the Gledhills.

The plan was that Joe Jr., who had taken a new job as a systems consultant with National Office Products Ltd. in nearby Dartmouth, would live in his childhood home for a time until he'd saved enough money to set up a new living arrangement closer to work. The arrangement required him to commute nearly an hour every morning and night the almost 68 kilometres between his parent's house in Chester and his job in Dartmouth. Out of concern for his son's safety, Joe Sr. purchased a gently used, 1988 Ford Mustang for Joe Jr. to replace his older, less reliable car. Joe Jr. was thrilled, but he wasn't someone who accepted that kind of help easily, and he insisted that he'd repay his father as soon as he was better established. Joe Jr. was considered hard-working, determined, family-centred and proud to all who knew him. It appeared he was happy, well adjusted and loved life and all the possibilities it held for his future.

By the morning of Tuesday, September 20, 1994, the Gledhills had established a new daily routine that, once again, included their only son. Morning chatter was typically filled with plans for the day, and mother Gledhill had promised her son a special treat for supper—Coq au Vin. The chicken dish was her son's favourite meal, and he voiced his pleasure at having a mouth-watering dinner to look forward to after a hard day at work.

The day progressed along its usual course. Marilyn tackled the typical chores, tidying the house and doing laundry, stopping long enough to enjoy the colourful tapestry of fall leaves flickering in the breeze outside her window. As promised, dinner was ready and waiting on the table by 6:30 that evening, its tempting aroma wafting through the house. This was the family's usual dinner hour, and Joe Jr. was usually home by that time. This evening, however, the planned festive weekday meal was getting cold as the minutes ticked along. By 7:00 PM, hunger pangs were replaced by worry as the Gledhills discussed their son's tardiness. It was uncharacteristically thoughtless of Joe Jr. to be late and not call home, and the lack of any communication whatsoever gave the Gledhills an uneasy feeling. Deciding to do a little sleuthing on their own, they checked to see if there were any traffic concerns along Highway 103, where Joe Jr. would have been driving. When this didn't turn up anything out of the ordinary, they went a step further, calling friends and family members to see if they'd heard from Joe Jr. None had.

By 8:30 PM Marilyn and Joe Sr. had forced down a bit of their supper, cleared the table and continued making phone calls, this time to local hospitals to see if anyone matching their son's description had checked in. Nothing. As a last resort, they called the Chester RCMP and Halifax and Dartmouth police departments. All three confirmed to the Gledhills that no accidents along the route Joe Jr. would have driven had been reported.

In a book entitled *Our Son Is Missing: The Story of a Six-Week Nightmare*, penned by the Gledhills, Marilyn remembers thinking they may have been hasty with their concern. Their son was a grown man and could have any number of reasons for being late that night. The self-admonishment obviously didn't sit well, as she goes on to explain how she and Joe Sr. climbed into the family car in the wee hours of September 21, retracing Joe Jr.'s daily commute. That excursion resulted in much of the same—nothing. At 9:00 AM the next day the Gledhills' worst fears were confirmed. Joe Sr. called his son's work and learned he hadn't clocked in the previous day, which meant by that point he'd been missing a full 24 hours.

They contacted the RCMP, other family members and close friends. Since no accidents of any significance involving a 1988 Mustang were reported in the area during the previous 24 hours, law enforcement personnel had to entertain the possibility that Joe Jr. had chosen to disappear. Typically respectful of her son's privacy, Marilyn, under the request of the RCMP, begrudgingly scoured Joe Jr.'s bedroom in search of names and phone numbers of his close friends or any other information she could uncover that might shed light on why her son would leave so abruptly.

At the same time, the thought of Joe Jr. taking off on purpose was never an option that she or her husband even considered. They knew their son. Not just like other folks say they know their children only to later discover all kinds of things they may not have known. No, the Gledhills knew Joe Jr. through and through. Their son had nothing to hide; the family was always open with each other no matter how difficult the topic of discussion. If Joe Jr. had been having problems, he would have confided in his parents, and together they'd have worked things out. That was the way it was in the Gledhill household.

However, faced with the more objective view of the RCMP—who gently explained that in their experience it wasn't uncommon for young folks going through a difficult time for one reason or another to leave for a few days—the Gledhills had to look at other options. They started questioning their interpretation of their son. Maybe he was troubled and didn't feel he could turn to them? Since their biggest fear was that Joe Jr. had been in an accident and was injured and alone somewhere, the alternative was disturbingly appealing. They started asking their friends and family for their thoughts on the matter. They called Joe Jr.'s friends, explaining the situation and begging for insight into their son's life. Their research only confirmed what the

Gledhills already knew—their son had no reason to leave without a word to his family.

There was one slight chink in the armour, however. An interview between the RCMP and Joe Jr.'s physician when he was living in Grand Falls, New Brunswick, revealed that Joe "could be moody…had difficulty with stress, and had consulted him about stress-related illness." The Gledhills were well aware of their son's job-related difficulties, caused to a large degree by a corporate takeover. Still, as Corporal Doug Grist, the RCMP officer sharing this newfound information with the Gledhills, gently suggested, the stress could explain Joe Jr.'s sudden absence. That realization, coupled with news reports where law enforcement officials repeatedly suggested they believed Joe was still alive, forced the reluctant Gledhills to consider the unthinkable. Perhaps Joe Jr. had chosen to leave, after all. And if that was the case, the Gledhills couldn't help but wonder how they might have missed signs of their son's possible discontent.

However unlikely the RCMP and other law enforcement officials may have thought it to be, all possible scenarios had to be investigated. Along with a plethora of volunteers giving their time to organize search parties—just in case the Gledhills were right and Joe Jr. had been in a terrible accident—and the RCMP's ongoing investigations, Marilyn and Joe Sr. floated through a haze. The couple feared that their son was dead. Yet they cautiously hoped that once a reported sighting was confirmed they would find their son still alive.

At one point, motivated by the kind of desperation only a parent can understand, the Gledhills even consulted a psychic. According to Marilyn's account, Evelyn Hare was as affable as she was friendly. Holding articles belonging to Joe Jr., she described a scene with a highway, brush, boulders and then darkness. She seemed to sense Joe Jr. may have crossed the centre lane and disappeared over the opposite shoulder. She described the scene as containing "large boulders, and trees hanging over the roadway," and then nothing. It was a scene that Marilyn and Joe Sr. would later discover was eerily accurate—but not before one eyewitness reported seeing their son "living with a prostitute" and "on drugs."

The roller coaster of emotions the Gledhills must have experienced throughout their six-week ordeal is unfathomable. Although they expected the worst, it was only natural to hope they were wrong. Yet despite planning yet another ground search armed with the psychic's vision and with the full expectation of finding their long-deceased son, learning the truth was still a cruel blow. Even though air and ground searches had been conducted, it wasn't until the fall had claimed most of the area's lush foliage that the accident scene was revealed. On October 31, 1994, Corporal Grist informed the Gledhills that their son's wreckage and his lifeless body had been spotted by a highway grader operator off "Highway 103 at Exit 6." Now the couple had to go from planning ground searches and praying for miracles to planning a funeral.

That their missing son was dead was now an indisputable fact. But it didn't answer all the questions. How could Joe Jr.'s Mustang tear across the centre lane of a busy highway during rush hour traffic and crash over the shoulder without anyone noticing? Is it possible someone may have noticed something out of the ordinary but thought it too insignificant to report? And what caused him to cross the centre line? Had he swerved to miss some wildlife?

The Gledhills did have one thought on how the accident could have happened. One year before Joe Jr.'s accident, two of his cousins, both around his age, died in the same week. An autopsy discovered that both young men, though appearing fit and healthy, suffered from a rare congenital heart condition called arrythmogenic right ventricular dysplasia. Medical tests further revealed that their siblings and their children all presented the condition, and just days before the accident, it was discovered that the disorder seemed to have stemmed from Marilyn's mother's side of the family. It was quite possible, then, that Joe Jr. suffered some kind of heart-related attack on the morning of the accident. Unfortunately, an autopsy conducted six weeks after Joe Jr.'s death wasn't able to confirm or deny such a condition.

One thing that haunts the Gledhills to this day, though, was the accident scene itself. Joe Jr. was found lying on his back outside the car, surrounded by large boulders and trees hanging over the roadway where it occurred, just as the psychic had predicted. But most disconcerting for the Gledhills was that the keys to the car were found in Joe Jr.'s shirt pocket, possibly revealing that he'd survived the accident, if only for a short time. Still, they had the small comfort of knowing what happened to their son and the chance to say goodbye with a proper burial. That's significantly more than the loved ones in this next story were able to secure. ∾

LOST BOYS

Sometimes reporting a concern before something happens is just as important as reporting it afterwards. Such was the case with a joyride gone sour more than a dozen years ago in the first few hours of Friday, March 17, 1995.

With the hint of spring just around the corner, Oshawa resident Michael Cummins (17), Pickering's Chad Smith (18), Jay Boyle (17) and Robbie Rumboldt (18) along with Jamie LeFebvre (17) of Scarborough and Danny Higgins (16) of Ajax were feeling a bit mischievous. And perhaps they grew a tad bored with the party they'd been attending that night. According to news reports in the *Toronto Sun*, Michael had stopped by his girlfriend's house with his buddies around 12:45 AM, telling her that he and his friends were hiking down to the Pickering waterfront. The only other sighting of any of the young men came from video footage that allegedly shows three youth "borrowing" two boats—a paddleboat from Swan's Marina and a fibreglass boat sporting a 25-horsepower motor from East Shore Marina. From there, the group simply vanished into the dark and murky waters of Lake Ontario—a lake that's well known for not giving up its dead.

The saying "Boys will be boys" may have never been a more suitable adage as it was in the case for these six young men, who were dubbed Ontario's "Lost Boys." Accounts given by family and friends seem to agree on several points. All six were basically good young men who were well liked by friends and considered close to their respective families. But they were young and adventurous and fun-loving, too, and they'd been known to push the envelope.

Perhaps it was the beer or two they each consumed at the party that fateful night that inevitably loosened their inhibitions and allowed them throw caution to the wind. Whatever led to their decision to board a stolen boat and venture out into a lake that's known for its unforgiving nature will never be known for sure. But for the most part, it was thought the youngsters were out for nothing more than a harmless joyride. Which of us, if we are being truthful, hasn't at least once bitten off a little more roguery than we could chew? And boys will be boys, after all.

The next morning, loved ones rose to the unsettling discovery that their sons and boyfriends were missing. Chad's girlfriend expected him home by 5:00 AM that Friday, but she rolled over to find his side of their bed empty. Jay's girlfriend Monique Vavala started out the day feeding the couple's four-month-old daughter Kierra and worrying about where Jay was. Fun-loving and mischievous he most certainly was, and although he was only 17, he had done everything he could to be a good father to his baby girl and not showing up the entire night was not at all like him. While the other families were learning their sons weren't home, phones among friends and family started ringing. Before long it was clear—all six boys were missing.

By early afternoon law enforcement were informed of the missing teens, and on Saturday, they began conducting air and ground searches. A Canadian Forces Hercules plane and Labrador helicopter joined three area police forces in that first effort. They searched marinas along the lakeshore for signs of the missing boat and asked neighbouring jurisdictions to search their marinas as well. Scores of area residents, including people who didn't know any of the missing teens, turned out in droves to join in the search. Not a scrap of evidence, aside from the foggy video, was ever discovered.

The story initially brought a variety of responses from the people who knew and loved the boys. One friend suggested that they may have ditched the boat somewhere and went partying in Toronto. Another hypothesis that rose was perhaps the youth had realized the recklessness of their behaviour and were afraid of the retribution they were sure to receive for "borrowing" the boats and joyriding and were hiding out somewhere. That the youth met with a fatal accident was the last option anyone wanted to consider. And most folks weren't ready to go in that direction just yet.

One strong fact that kept hope alive for friends and families of the lost boys was the kind of boat they were suspected of having "borrowed"—a replica of a Boston Whaler. The original Boston Whaler was developed and built by Richard "Dick" Fisher and Raymond Hunt in 1956. Fisher is credited with creating a virtually unsinkable boat. He demonstrated his claim, making it an indisputable fact, when *Life Magazine* featured his product in their May 19, 1961 issue. The story is accompanied by a photo showing Fisher sitting near the boat's motor while the boat is being sawed in half. Once the boat was in two complete pieces, Fisher used his half to tow the other half to shore. Neither sank in the process. Surely a boat built with similar qualities to the original Boston Whaler wouldn't be found at the bottom of Lake Ontario. And yet no trace of it was to be found.

As the searches continued, crowds gathered at the site where the boys were last thought to have been. Schoolmates joined in with 16-year-old Amanda Boyle, Jay's sister, as she tied yellow ribbons to a nearby willow tree. Other friends and family members visited the area throughout the days following the disappearance, huddling together for support and whispering prayer after prayer for a happy ending. A week of air, water and ground searches had been conducted, and 2000 volunteers scoured the shoreline from Oshawa to Mississauga. Still nothing. Against official advice, complete strangers ventured out onto the lake to see if they could find anything. Again, no go.

Although no signs of the boys washed ashore, families still rode the highs and lows of suspected sightings and subsequent disappointments. Early on in the investigation, an abandoned boat was found in the Ajax marsh area, but it was quickly ruled out as the boat the boys were suspected of having used. At one point, police received a call that someone had sighted something in the lake that looked like a body. Unfortunately, by the time police got out on the water, whatever it was had disappeared. Almost three months after the teens disappeared, a concerned fisherman thought he'd spotted a body floating near Frenchman's Bay and, using his fish finder, he also believed he may have discovered a submerged boat about one kilometre from shore. Police divers found no evidence of a body, but they did locate a large boat-shaped rock on the lake bottom.

Of all the assorted caps, pieces of clothing and other personal items collected during the numerous ground searches, none was linked to the young men. The only piece of evidence recovered from the suspected mishap was the boat's gas can. At some point it washed ashore near Wilson, New York, almost directly south of Pickering.

It was widely reported that there were no life jackets or oars on board the boat and only about a half a tank of gas—not enough to travel more than 25 to 40 kilometres. Is it possible, once they ran out of gas, the teens simply drifted onto foreign soil? Could they have been picked up by someone in another vessel? Is it possible they were all victims of foul play? Could they have survived an accident and lost their memories, carrying on with new lives in another land? Or had the boat simply over-turned, tossing the young men into the near-freezing waters of Lake Ontario? If so, experts estimate the boys would have suc-cumbed to hypothermia within a few short minutes, and the cold temperature of the lake would prevent the natural stomach gases in the bodies from releasing and, therefore, trap the bodies underwater.

Since that fateful night, friends and family members have gathered around the willow tree with the now long-since faded yellow ribbons. For the first few years, the families would meet on the anniversary of the disappearance. At other times they'd gather in smaller groups, remembering a birthday or what would have been some other special milestone for their loved one. But no matter what, no one who cared for these boys has had closure, and the drive to discover what transpired that night hasn't dimmed.

In early 2006, perhaps in an attempt to gather new or previously unreported information on the vanished teens, one friend, who has chosen to remain anonymous "so the focus stays on (his) missing friends," produced a video called "lostboys1995" for the Internet site "YouTube." A collection of news snippets and personal photos of the missing boys make up the majority of the five-minute film, and the responses to it indicate those close to the boys are pleased with the memorial. "I'm Siobhan, Jay's lil sister," one entry reads. "I want to thank the person who made this. It's very touching. We all love and miss him sooooo much…"

A *Toronto Sun* news story printed on the 12th anniversary of the Lost Boys saga highlights the efforts of another friend to find answers. Roxanne Griffin approached the Women's Entertainment Network television show *Rescue Mediums* in an attempt to garner the expertise of the show's two acclaimed psychics, Christine Hamlett and Jackie Dennison, and to take advantage of the media exposure the show would provide. It's not the first time these British psychics have been approached to solve a Canadian cold case. The two women covered the stories of Ontario's Lois Hanna and Nova Scotia's Rhonda Wilson in past episodes. At this point it's not certain if the Lost Boys will be featured in the future or not, but Griffin isn't daunted.

"C'mon, not a shoe, a boot or a hat? Nothing has ever showed up," Griffin said in the March 17, 2007, *Toronto Sun* report. "These poor families. All I want is closure for these families."

Closure. That's all anyone involved in this or any other missing persons case wants. And until something concrete is discovered that makes closure possible, friends and families of the Lost Boys will continue to hope, to pray and to meet on the shores of Lake Ontario. ❧

STOPPING TO SMELL THE ROSES

Robert Frost said it best in his much-loved poem *The Road Not Taken*. While it's fine to hike along well-worn pathways, the really wonderful surprises in life are often just a stone's throw away, perhaps hidden in the underbrush or past that clump of trees to your right. That's where the blueberries are plumper, the wildflowers more plentiful and the scent of green all the more heavenly. If you add our natural human curiosity to the mix, it's no stretch to imagine wandering a few steps farther so that you can perch atop a granite cliff to take in the view. Before you know it, you've lost all sense of direction—and which granite cliff were you standing on anyway? It's just this kind of scenario that is behind a great many of the missing persons reported each year. And it's exactly what happened to 72-year-old Garry Linde of Breton, Alberta, in the early days of December 2005.

The word "senior" didn't describe how Garry felt from day to day. Unhampered by his age, Garry carried on with his daily activities like a gent half his age. And on Thursday, December 9, the main chore on his mind was a trip to the local dump. Hopping into his dark grey, 1999 Chevy Silverado truck, already packed with the refuse needing transport, Garry nodded a goodbye to his wife Leona and headed out. With her own chores to do, it was a while before Leona noticed that her husband had been gone a considerably long time. Perhaps he'd met some of his buddies for coffee and, well, you know how men can talk.

But as the afternoon wore on, with darkness rapidly replacing daylight, Leona was no longer just concerned, she was considerably alarmed. At 11:00 PM she contacted the RCMP, and the search for the missing man began.

Spending a winter night outside, even in a vehicle, isn't a good idea in the best of circumstances. Winters in Alberta can be ruthless. Temperatures in early December can plummet well below zero, and with wind chill, much lower. And chances were that Garry hadn't equipped his truck with an emergency kit since he only ever used it for chores, and he'd had every intention of being in his nice, warm bed that night.

As the next day dawned and there was still no sign of Garry, family members really began to worry. How long could he last in the cold without food or water? Sure, he was a feisty old guy, but still, even hardy men of much younger stock would find a night in the cold challenging. While the Linde family were pacing, searching and praying, the world around them was preparing for the festive Christmas season. There'd be no Christmas for the Lindes if Garry wasn't found. The family simply wouldn't have the stomach for it.

Saturday came to a close, then Sunday, and just when all hope of finding Garry alive and well was lost, he and his truck were discovered on Monday. It appeared he hadn't even made it to the dump, deciding to venture off in search of a Christmas tree instead. Although he managed to find and cut down the perfect tree to grace the Lindes' home that festive season, when he turned the truck around, he got stuck. Unable to free it, Garry stayed with the vehicle that first night. But when he heard a news report about his misadventure, he decided to try hiking home. He didn't make it far before he had to stop for a rest. He was discovered by a friend, taken to hospital and treated for little more than hypothermia. The Linde family was lucky indeed. Theirs would be a truly blessed Christmas season.

For 77-year-old John Jack Ryan, the end result of a terrifying nine-day search wouldn't end as happily. On Thursday, March 11, 1993, the elderly grandfather started out the day completing his usual routine. By 8:00 AM he had already dropped off his wife Jeanne at Commerce Court in Toronto, as well as taken his daughter, K.C. Ryan, to Bloor and Bathurst streets. Then there was the daily pit stop at Johnny's Donuts for a coffee and chatter with the fellows. His wife and family wouldn't know until hours later that he'd never made it for his morning coffee, but by that evening, police and family were actively searching for the missing man. And the quest to find John was made more urgent when it was revealed that he suffered from several physical ailments that required ongoing medication, all of which were still in his East York home.

As the search intensified, the media issued a public plea for any information on the missing grandfather. Posters with his photograph were distributed, and police followed up on suspected sightings. One individual reported seeing the man in the

Barrie area three days after John had gone missing. This was a particularly promising clue, because the family had a cabin in the area, and John would have travelled that route should he have changed his plans and decided on a trip to the cottage. Unfortunately, the tip, like so many others, turned out to be a red herring.

Meanwhile, police and volunteers carried out ground searches in and around the city, and a helicopter search was also conducted. Nine days after John's disappearance, it was a pedestrian walking by John's Chrysler Dynasty on Shutter Street who noticed an elderly fellow slumped over the steering wheel and called police. It appears John had pulled over for a moment and died in his car. A sad ending for the Ryan family, but at least they were able to bring their loved one home to say goodbye.

~

For the family of 70-year-old Marjorie Amy Ferris, however, the mystery continues.

Marjorie was an active and outgoing senior who appeared much younger than her 70 years. Although she was widowed, that didn't stop her from enjoying life to its fullest. From her apartment on Burlington's Lakeshore Road, she regularly took brisk walks around the Lake Ontario shoreline. Not only did these jaunts keep Marjorie healthy and vibrant, they also allowed her to feed the geese from a bag of assorted treats she always brought along.

Thursday, March 5, 1993, was much like any other busy day for Marjorie. She was looking forward to her trip to London, Ontario, that weekend. She was visiting friends there, and they were all planning to drive down to Florida. At around 10:00 PM that night, Marjorie was seen by her neighbours as they all gathered in the apartment building's lobby for a routine fire drill. She appeared to be her usual cheerful self and was quite excited about her upcoming trip. But when she never arrived in London, and her friends were unable to contact her, concerns over her well-being were raised.

Because Marjorie lived alone, her son Robert checked her suite. What he found when he entered the locked apartment only concerned him further. Everything was as it should be. Marjorie's purse was in its usual place on a bedside chair, her wallet and American money was intact on the dining room table, her chequebook and a rent cheque sat in plain sight. Her car keys hung in their usual place, and her car was safely parked in the apartment's underground garage. Marjorie, however, was nowhere to be found.

Adding to the strange disappearance was that Marjorie's coats were hanging in her closet. It appeared as if the bird lover may have ventured off just in her winter boots—a strange possibility, according to her 85-year-old neighbour Edith Crittle. She "was far too sensible to go out without her coat," Edith told *Toronto Sun* reporters.

During the next three weeks, Marjorie's routine walking paths were searched—the Burlington waterfront, the neighbourhood surrounding her apartment, the entire apartment building. Even a helicopter search was conducted. But all these efforts failed to produce any trace of the woman. Had she been drawn to the lake, captivated by the fierce winds thrusting waves wildly against the shoreline and drowned, as one police detective speculated? It seemed the most likely answer to the mystery, but without a body to confirm that theory, her family still wonders what happened to her.

Chapter Nine

In the Spotlight

The arena of missing persons covers a wide array of possibilities behind their disappearance. Some individuals go missing quite unintentionally. Perhaps they've taken a hike through the backwoods, something they've done a thousand times before, but for some reason or other, become disoriented and get lost. Other individuals may have been in the wrong place at the wrong time and were abducted by complete strangers. And then there are those cases that by the very mystery shrouding them, simply defy description.

Some cases are surrounded by such extremely unusual circumstances that all questions concerning the disappearance remain unanswered. In fact, when called upon for his services in one case, old Sherlock Holmes (or at least his creator, Sir Arthur Conan Doyle) couldn't even solve the puzzle. In other cases it's not the disappearance that's the mystery so much as why the individual chose to vanish or what he or she hoped to gain by doing so. In every case, the stories that follow prove the old adage that truth is, indeed, stranger than fiction. ∾

HE SHOOTS, HE SCORES!

Long before the advent of summer hockey camps and personal trainers, youngsters who dreamed of becoming professional hockey players honed their skills on the backyard pond. Equipped with nothing more than old Eaton's or Sears' catalogues strapped to their shins with baling twine, an old broom handle or tree branch for a stick and cow patties for hockey pucks, kids spent hours drawing lots to form teams and challenging each other in tournaments of their own making. Such an environment wasn't far off from how William Barilko got his start in the sport.

Born in Timmins, Ontario, on March 25, 1927, the youngster of Ukrainian descent had a few obstacles to overcome if he were to make it to the NHL some day. Kevin Shea, author of *Barilko: Without a Trace,* describes how the shy young man, soon to be known as "Bashin' Bill" Barilko, came from a poor family, didn't own any hockey equipment, was far from the best skater in the world and had terrible eyesight to boot—but he had a lot of heart. "He found his way, miraculously and against all odds, to the NHL," Shea said in an interview with freelance writer Michael Boon. "Dreams can come true. Bill Barilko proved it."

Yes, Bill proved hard work and determination paid off. He wasn't yet 20 when the defenceman was called up from the Hollywood Wolves as an injury replacement for the Toronto Maple Leafs in February 1947. Standing a full 180 centimetres (5 feet 11 inches) in height, and weighing in at 83 kilograms (184 pounds) of solid muscle, Bashin' Bill soon earned his nickname, bodychecking his opponents out of the way so that the team's key goal scorers had a clear shot at the net and gaining the respect of his coaches and fellow players. That season, which marked his first in the NHL, he played 11 playoff games, assisted in three goals and proudly took his place with his team members as they accepted the Stanley Cup that year.

Bashin' Bill remained part of the Leafs for the next four remarkable seasons, helping them earn three more Stanley Cups. In a total of 252 games played throughout his career, he scored 26 goals and earned 36 assists. He also racked up 456 penalty minutes, which, if you're into numbers, is almost one two-minute penalty per game. But Bill's claim to fame occurred on April 21, in the dying minutes of game five of the 1951 Stanley Cup final. Facing off against the Montréal Canadiens, with talent the likes of Maurice Richard in their lineup, the Leafs jumped ahead to a remarkable 3–1 series lead. All four games had been decided in overtime play, and game five was no different. As usual, Bill's job was to "bodycheck guys into oblivion" as Jack Batten put it in his book *The Leafs*. But at 2:53 into the second period, something happened—call it a gut reaction, instinct, reflex or whatever—and Bill leapt into action. He charged from his appointed spot on the Canadiens blue line, eyes fixated on the loose puck rebounding in front of the Montréal net, and backhanded it over the shoulder of netminder Gerry McNeil. In 46 previous playoff games, Bashin' Bill had only scored four goals, but on that April day, he was a hero to every Toronto Maple Leaf fan across the country.

As the summer of 1951 neared, Bill couldn't feel happier with his life. The adrenalin rush he got from that Stanley Cup Final–winning goal would easily carry him through the summer and into the next hockey season. But first, a short break was in order, and a fishing trip to James Bay was just what he needed. Accompanied by his friend Dr. Henry Hudson, Bill was anxious to see if his luck with a lure was anywhere as successful as his luck with the puck. Really though, even if there were only a few tugs on the line that warm August day, the clear blue lakes, the sound of the loon and the feel of a cool summer breeze made the trip north more than worth it. By the time the two men boarded Hudson's Fairchild 24 floatplane to return home, Mother Nature had successfully completed her rejuvenation program, and both were well rested and ready to leave. It had been four months and five days since Bill was last on the ice, and training camp would be starting any day.

During that trip home, however, the plane, along with the promising young hockey player and his friend, vanished somewhere between Rupert House and Timmins. When neither man returned home, massive search efforts were organized, and the flight path it was thought Hudson took was scoured. But there was no sign of the plane or its occupants.

People being people, tongues tend to wag, and minds wander where they will. Perhaps it was sheer denial that first fed the rumours, but the mill started turning nonetheless. One story suggested Bill's plane never crashed at all, but instead, the skilled player had defected and was actually sharing his talents with budding hockey stars in Russia.

Eleven long years passed. When it came to winning Stanley Cups, the Toronto Maple Leafs experienced a drought during that entire time. And then, in early June 1962, a bush pilot named Gary Fields was flying around the area south of James Bay and about 100 kilometres north of Cochrane when he spotted something in the bushes below. It was the Fairchild 24. The long-since missing Bill Barilko and his friend could finally come home to rest. Oddly enough, the year of his home-coming signified the first time since his disappearance that his beloved team won another Stanley Cup, further cementing his image in Maple Leaf and NHL history.

In his honour, on October 17, 1992, Bill Barilko's number 5 jersey joined Ace Bailey's number 6 jersey as both were retired that day. They remain the only two numbers the team has retired in its entire 90-year history. ❧

HISTORY IN ICE

Fishing is a fine pastime, but during the off-season, snowboarding was more Duncan MacPherson's style. Duncan was a native of Saskatoon and had already made his mark as a strong defenceman, having earned the title of "most valuable defenceman" for North Battleford in the previous 1982–83 hockey season. Despite being out with an ankle injury for part of the next season, Duncan not only recovered but also was talented enough to make it to the big leagues, and in the fall of 1984 was picked up by the New York Islanders. He was just 18 years old.

The next two years would have him honing his skills in the American Hockey League with the Islanders' minor league team, the Springfield Indians, in Massachusetts. Although known as a hard hitter and a determined and focused player, Duncan never made it to NHL ice. Instead, he followed up his stint with the Indians with six months in the International Hockey League and was eventually offered a job as a player-coach with the Dundee Tigers in Dundee, Scotland. In the summer of 1989, the 23-year-old realized he needed to re-evaluate his options. Did he want to leave his family and friends in Canada and live in Scotland, or should he return home and re-examine his options there? He decided to take a short trip to visit a few friends to think about things for a few days.

With several friends and former teammates making their livelihoods elsewhere in Europe, Duncan had no shortage of opinions to garner. In early August 1989 he visited former NHL player George Pesut in Nuremberg, Germany. Also a native of Saskatoon, Pesut at that time was playing for a Nuremberg team and scheduled to head out to Prague, Czechoslovakia, for a tournament. Pesut offered his car to Duncan while he was away. Excited at the prospect of a set of wheels to tour the countryside, Duncan first headed out to Fussen to visit another former teammate named Roger Kortko. From there he had planned to travel to Italy for a couple of days and then return his loaner car on August 10. But somewhere along the way, he changed his mind, his imagination likely captured by the magnificent scenery surrounding him, and he ended up on an Austrian ski slope on August 9. Fresh powder and the rush of a good run should clear his head and help him focus on his future—and apparently it had. The next day he called the president of the Dundee Tigers saying he'd accept the job offer and would arrive in Scotland on the 12th. He explained that after he dropped off his loaner car in Nuremberg, he'd ride the train to Frankfurt and fly in from there. But a little more of that fresh powder, first.

Duncan never arrived in Scotland, nor did he contact the Dundee Tigers again. And his friend George, who'd arrived back home on August 15, noticed Duncan's luggage still in his apartment and his car still gone. It was clear to all who knew Duncan that something was very wrong. Police were contacted, missing persons reports filed in West Germany and Canada, and a search begun, but where in-between Nuremberg and Italy could he have come into harm's way? Investigators, along with Duncan's parents, Bob and Lynda, his brother Derrick, and

Duncan's girlfriend arrived in West Germany on August 28, would have to retrace his steps to uncover the mystery.

It wasn't until September 20, 1989, after the MacPhersons had managed to influence an Austrian television station to broadcast the story of their son's disappearance and to show a picture of the car he was driving that the family received their first real break in the case. An employee of the Stubai Glacier Ski Resort recognized the car as the one that for weeks had been sitting in their parking lot. When investigators and Duncan's kin arrived at the resort, ski instructor Walter Hinterholzl recognized the photograph on the missing person's poster that the MacPhersons had taped to their car window. He soon explained to investigators that he had tutored the young hockey player on August 9, after which the pair had lunch together. Duncan had booked another lesson for the following day and then headed back out to the practice slopes to try putting into action his newly acquired skills. The ski instructor then stated that Duncan never showed up for his lesson the next day, and records from the rental shop seemed to indicate that he had turned in all his equipment. If that was true, what could have become of the 23-year-old between the rental office and the parking lot?

By this time, a missing person's report had been filed in Austria. Alpine rescue volunteers and police searched the ski hill. A Canadian search team arrived on the scene on October 8 and joined in the searches, but when nothing turned up by

October 14, the search was called off and, reluctantly, the MacPhersons returned home.

Bob and Lynda returned to Austria the following year in July 1990, concerned about how the investigation into Duncan's disappearance had been handled. In their return visit to the Stubai Glacier Ski Resort, they happened to notice a woman who, without the quick reaction of her ski partner to save her, would have fallen through a snow bridge covering a crevasse. It was a scene they were to remember many years later.

Meanwhile, weeks turned into months and years, but Duncan's parents were relentless. They continued trying to get the word out about their missing son, and in August 1993 his story aired on a German television program. Six months later, on February 9, 1994, a man named Mark Schoffman was claiming to have amnesia. Authorities believed he matched Duncan's description. Could it be that after all these years the MacPhersons would be reunited with their son? Unfortunately, that was not the case.

Another nine years dragged on, until Mother Nature herself intervened. Inordinately warm weather had melted considerable portions of the snow at the Stubai Glacier Ski Resort, and on July 18, 2003, an employee of the resort noticed something out of the ordinary. On closer inspection, he found the body of a young man encased in ice and frozen in time. It was at the exact location where in 1990 Bob and Lynda had witnessed the young woman who had almost fallen through the crevasse of a snow bridge! At long last the mystery of what became of young Duncan MacPherson was solved.

There are still many questions surrounding the MacPherson tragedy—questions that likely keep members of Duncan's family up at night. But at least they can take some measure of comfort in knowing their son is now home, where he belongs. ∽

NO SMALL STORY

This tale has all the markings of a Hollywood movie—the dashing prince charming who's more of a curmudgeon than most would like to admit, the millionaire missus who keeps her man in check with her cheque book and a love for the theatre and all things dramatic. The story of Ambrose Small and his disappearance in 1919 had been called the "Crime of the Century" by news outlets around the world at that time. His story has puzzled the police for decades, fuelling stories and documentaries and generally leaving folks scratching their heads in wonder.

Ambrose Small wasn't a nice man. But by all accounts he started out on the right path, labouring at his father's Warden Hotel in Toronto at the young age of 13 and climbing his way up the ladder to a management position in the hotel bar. He also worked part time as an usher for London's Grand Theatre. Here again he worked his way into management and in a short time was made responsible for filling the theatre's line up of entertainment.

At the same time, Small had bigger plans—plans that needed larger quantities of cash than his present jobs could provide. Not a problem, for Small took to gambling but not in a small or always legitimate way. Although he was known to always pay his debts, he more often won money than not. He was also a renowned womanizer, boasting a buxom beauty clinging to one arm or the other, and sometimes even both. So it was surprising at first, when in 1902 at the age of 39, he announced he was now a married man. Of course, when the identity of his new bride was revealed, it made all the sense in the world, because the new Mrs. Theresa Small was a wealthy heiress. It wasn't long before the newlyweds used some of that money to buy small theatres, and lots of them, and to bring in some high-priced talent. Small already owned London's Grand Theatre by then, but Theresa's money meant he could start living his dreams and put gambling and womanizing on the backburner—at least for a time.

A little exploration into Theresa's life and personality can't help but leave one bewildered. She appeared to be a pillar of morality and a staunch Catholic with a propensity for charitable works and a heart for the less fortunate. Yet her marriage to Small had to indicate another side to the woman. He was her polar opposite, openly denouncing children, Catholics and the poor equally. To Small's way of thinking, if someone was down on their luck, it was likely because they deserved it.

So what drew these two unlikely souls together? A casual observer could follow the money from Small to Theresa and make a link that way. But why was she attracted to him? There must have been something in it for the heiress, because the couple, happily or not, remained married for 17 years. Then on December 2, 1919, Ambrose J. Small disappeare into a blustery Toronto night, never to be seen or heard from again.

Perhaps it was because Small picked up his old gambling habits and took on at least one mistress, but whatever the reason, at the time of his disappearance, the couple had begun to tire of the entertainment industry. The day Small went missing, the two had signed a deal to sell their chain of theatres to a British interest and sealed the deal by accepting a $1 million cheque as a down payment. In their investigations, police confirmed the cheque had been deposited in the couple's Dominion Bank account before noon that day. Shortly thereafter, Small's attorney reported speaking with his client, and just around the supper hour, Small was seen by Ralph Savein, an entrepreneur operating the newsstand on the corner of Adelaide and Yonge streets. As was his habit, Small wanted to check the day's horseracing results, but the paper hadn't been delivered due to the stormy weather conditions, and Small trudged away sounding his disappointment. The police confirmed that Savein was the last person who spoke with Small.

That Small's mysterious disappearance went unreported for several days didn't initially raise any suspicion. After all, he marched to his own drummer, and it wasn't uncommon for him to take off from time to time to indulge in an all-out gambling and carousing spree. But once a report was made and police started investigating, a few tips led them and the public to suspect Small had been murdered. On reflecting on the night of December 2, a witness named George Soucy reported he thought he saw Small being muscled into a vehicle. Another report from a gent named Albert Elson suggested someone was burying something out in back of the Small's family home that same evening. And a cleaning lady recalled seeing a notice requesting prayers for the recently departed Small at the Convent of Precious Blood church long before news of his disappearance had hit the papers.

These reports may not have been enough to lead to the immediate conviction of any one suspect, but they certainly led to what was dubbed by the media of the day as "one of the biggest manhunts in Canadian history." The entire city of Toronto was searched, along with every city where the Smalls owned a theatre. Walls and floorboards were dismantled; Small's family basement as well as that of the Grand Opera House were dug up; Toronto Bay was dredged; and even the Grand Theatre's old furnace was searched in the hope of finding a splinter of bone that could have possibly belonged to the missing man. It was like a proverbial search for gold, without discovering pyrite. No clues were ever uncovered.

One might wonder how the bereaved Mrs. Small was holding up through it all. Despite her impeccable reputation, some folks started pointing fingers her way. She was accused of living off the proceeds of her husband's illicit entertainment industry, which, by then, was earning a reputation as little more than an early-day porn theatre and strip club. Rumours of a secret sex hideaway built into the Grand Theatre to accommodate Small and his many mistresses fuelled the theory that Theresa might have done away with her no-good husband. Nasty photos of Theresa look-alikes posing in unladylike positions with men and women of the cloth were also distributed, all of which prevented the bereaved Mrs. Small from getting her hands on what was left of the couple's fortune.

Apparently, Theresa's Catholic leanings conflicted with the Protestant powers in office at that time, and they opposed her inheritance, using everything they could to suggest she'd be profiting from the proceeds of a crime. It took a 15-year court battle, but eventually her name was cleared, and wherever her husband was buried, he must have rolled over in his grave when in 1935 she willed her estate to the Catholic Church.

Theresa died in 1936, but that didn't stop the rumour mill from churning regarding her or her wayward husband. One source suggested that evidence pointing to Theresa's involvement in his disappearance was intentionally suppressed. And long after Small was considered dead, Toronto police still received reports of folks spotting the maverick alive and well in exotic locales as far away as South America and France. Even the famed Sir Arthur Conan Doyle, intrigued with the mystery on hearing of it early in 1920 and who while touring the United States was interviewed by the press, agreed to lend his deductive abilities to the case should the authorities approach him to do so, but apparently they never did. After all, without a body, reported sightings of Small couldn't be completely ignored, even though he was officially declared dead in 1923.

Dead or not, police continued to investigate the cold case. Tips and letters continued to trickle in. Some were hoaxes while others were legitimate-sounding enough that yet another possible burial site would be unearthed. After the Toronto Police Department officially closed the files on the case in 1960, they still often followed up leads. In one instance in 1965, a suspected gravesite in Rosedale Valley was investigated. The story of Ambrose J. Small had clearly taken on mythic proportions. In a way, the theatre magnate became in death what he never completely achieved in life—he was the star of his own story.

Apparently he was a stubborn sort too, not wanting to abandon his much-loved Grand Theatre. As early as 1940, reports that the London landmark was haunted by Small's ghost were well established, though many folks claimed to have seen him wandering the stage started long before that. In May 1927, Toronto comedian Beatrice Lillie announced she'd seen Small calling to her, just one of the many performers who said they'd spotted his ghostly image throughout the years. Almost 90 years

have passed since that stormy day in December, but specula-
tions of what happened to Small still surface, and the story has
become fodder for all sorts of mystery and paranormal buffs,
likely stimulating imaginations for decades to come. ∾

MILLIONAIRE MYSTERY

To all outward appearances, Moe Jiwani had it all: money, and
lots of it, a beautiful doting wife, two adorable youngsters,
a mansion right on the shores of Lake Ontario and a corporate
career that included partnerships in hotels in Niagara Falls,
Winnipeg and London. But as they say, outward appearances
can be deceiving. And the Jiwani family was about to be thrust
into a mystery of unimagined proportions.

It all began one day in April 2006. Forty-one-year-old
hotelier Moe Jiwani explained to his wife Laila that he'd be
driving up to Toronto from their Oakville-area home that day
to attend a business meeting. When he didn't return home that
night, Laila may have been concerned, but not overly so, given
that four days passed before she finally reported her husband
missing.

Her hesitancy in calling police may have partly stemmed
from a similar experience she had two years earlier. At that time,
Moe Jiwani had disappeared for exactly four days before turning up at the Sandbar Tavern in Hamilton, a now defunct night-
spot with a wicked reputation involving drugs, crack dealers, at

least two homicides and several stabbings. The rumour at the time of his discovery was that Moe Jiwani wasn't exactly walking the straight and narrow when it came to drugs and alcohol, a suggestion Laila vehemently continues to deny.

Regardless the reason for her delay, once she reported him missing, his abandoned silver 2003 Mercedes was discovered in a parking lot in a less than favourable part of the big TO, a press release was issued about the story and missing person's posters plastered throughout the city. However glitzy and glamorous the story seemed, it produced only the slightest trickle of interest. The *Oakville Beaver* published a snippet on the vanished businessman on April 21, and the *Toronto Sun*'s Mark Bonokoski followed the story shortly thereafter and throughout the sordid tale. CTV picked up the mystery in December 2006, but otherwise, media were quite mute on the matter—more than just a little unsettling when you think about it.

Meanwhile, the days ticked along, and Moe remained on the missing person's list. In the hope of assisting the investigation, Laila hired private detectives Mark Mendelson and Mike Davis. Both retired homicide detectives, the pair has been following up on leads since the story first broke, but like the Toronto police, they just keep coming up cold.

About a month after Moe vanished, Laila was contacted by two men demanding $80,000 in ransom money for the safe return of her husband. Laila, threatened with her husband's safety, had to swear to keep the deal secret. She and her husband's partner, Ataf Mohamed, collected the money and took it to the Rexdale-area parking lot as they were directed. Money changed hands, and they were told to wait for two hours and then call a pre-paid cell phone for directions to Moe's whereabouts. When they made the call, the line was dead. That's when the pair finally called the police.

It took several months of investigative work before police felt they had enough on 26-year-old Sandor Richard Gelesics and 30-year-old Abdul Bashir (a one-time friend of the Jiwanis) to issue a search warrant and charge the two men with the alleged extortion of the $80,000.

As of this writing, no further information has been uncovered regarding the missing millionaire, and as more time passes, the higher the likelihood foul play is somehow involved. Moe Jiwani disappeared without a trace, and his family has yet to get the closure they so desperately seek.

"This is one huge stumper, no question about it," Mark Mendelson said in the *Toronto Sun*. "Laila Jiwani has not given up hope. She wants her husband back, and she would relish him coming home under any circumstances—regardless of how bad the story might be." ∞

In Disguise

For 21-year-old Pierre Mercon, October 31, 1996, was a day to celebrate. He'd just successfully completed a federal job-training program and was expecting a hefty cheque for his efforts. The next night was Friday, the day after Halloween, and parties were being hosted everywhere. Pierre had a hankering to let loose a little. His buddies were planning on taking in a Halloween party at the Original Six Sports Bar in Toronto's Richmond Hill area, and Pierre thought he'd tag along. It had been years since he'd dressed up for Halloween. It'll be fun, he thought as he rummaged through his family's home, piecing together a make-shift costume for the night.

Although he was certainly old enough to carry a driver's licence and motor his own way to the bar, Pierre was a responsible sort. He knew he'd be putting back a few, and drinking and driving wasn't his thing. Calling a buddy or taking a cab wasn't necessary, either. Pierre still lived at home, and his mother Norma offered to drive him down to the bar and pick him up later that night. So after he gathered together the collection of items he'd use to transform himself from the well-ordered, professional young fellow he was into a hippie for the night, Norma did exactly that. As he opened the car door and rose to leave, Pierre turned for a moment, thanked his mom and went off for a night on the town. It would be the last time Norma would set eyes on her son.

With more than 200 patrons venturing in and out of the now defunct Original Six, York police had a lot of people to interview once Pierre was reported missing. Pierre stood 180 centimetres (5 feet 11 inches) in height, and weighed about 100 kilograms (220 pounds). He had hazel eyes, brown hair, a dashing smile and a tattoo of Uruguay on his right shoulder. The trouble was that no one seemed to remember anything of significance when it came to the young man. The good news was that it meant Pierre hadn't been in some kind of altercation at the bar. The bad news was that he'd likely been approached in an area with few witnesses to observe anything.

With the information provided by Pierre's mother, police knew the young man had donned army fatigues, work boots, a green wool hat and a long black wig in an effort to transform himself for the night. They knew he was wearing a poncho, which was later discovered under what was thought to be the table where Pierre and his buddies were sitting. They also knew that at around last call, Pierre telephoned his mother from a pay phone outside the bar in the wee hours of November 2, asking her to meet him at the corner of Elgin Mills Road and Yonge Street. When she arrived just a few minutes later, her son was nowhere to be seen. She waited a while, toured around the club for a few blocks, but no Pierre. For all intents and purposes, Pierre Mercon quite literally seemed to have vanished.

Surely, it could be reasoned, if a young man chose to go missing, the last thing he'd do is call for a ride home and then not show up at the predetermined meeting location. It made no sense. As well, Pierre had no previous involvement with the police, not even a speeding ticket, and was considered a family-centred son who got along well with his parents and hadn't so much as sneezed out of line. The whole thing was like a bizarre, horrible nightmare without the promise of a new day to wash away the bad dream.

With the investigation stalled, a $25,000 reward was posted in December 1998 for information leading to Pierre Mercon's whereabouts. Two years later, that reward was doubled, but even a $50,000 reward hasn't managed to coax anyone forward. If someone knew something of value but wasn't coming forward, the person was either the reason for Pierre's disappearance or an extremely frightened witness. Either way, Pierre's family hangs on to the hope that someone, somewhere who saw something will someday share that information. Until then, only the memory of a loving, loyal son remains. ∿

THE CASE OF MR. NOBODY

After waking from a fitful sleep on a sunny Sunday morning in Toronto, most of us would have a few ideas on how we might spend the day. Perhaps a lunch date with an old friend is in order. Or since it's late November, why not get a jump on the upcoming holiday season and do a wee bit of Christmas shopping? Or how about taking in a Sunday stroll along Toronto's harbour front? It is Toronto, after all, so there's never a shortage of things to do.

But life is never really that simple, is it? And for one young man believed to be visiting the city, November 28, 1999, would definitely be a day to remember. In a way, that Sunday would signify the first day of the rest of his life.

News reports vary on the details surrounding the discovery of a man in Toronto General Hospital, but they all agree the lad, believed to be in his early 20s, showed up there after receiving a serious beating. Police were immediately called in on the case in the hope of finding the perpetrator responsible for such a brutal act. The trouble was, police couldn't get anywhere close to uncovering clues as to the incident, because the victim in this case wasn't very cooperative. It wasn't that he didn't want to help the police, it was just that when they asked him about what happened, he honestly didn't have a clue. In fact, he couldn't even remember his name, where he was, where he came from or anything about his life.

The unknown man, later dubbed "Mr. Nobody" by some media outlets, had suffered a concussion and for a time drifted in and out of consciousness. Doctors also diagnosed him as having global amnesia—a type of amnesia where a patient can recall what's happening from the time he regains consciousness, has the ability to walk, talk, write and can carry out activities of daily living but has neither a memory of the trauma suffered nor any idea of who he is. Most cases of global amnesia are transient, meaning that they usually last less than 24 hours. In Mr. Nobody's case, his amnesia appeared to be a permanent result of his beating.

Shortly after his initial admission to hospital, Mr. Nobody blurted out a name—Philip Staufen. Strangely enough, after a little research, it was discovered that Staufen was once the name of a medieval German king also known as Philip of Swabia (1177–1208). The patient was thereafter referred to as "Philip," and once DNA and fingerprint samples were collected, along with his photo, height, weight and his newly acquired identity, the information was circulated to law enforcement officials around the world.

The case garnered a fair amount of media attention. Because of his heavy British accent, which one University of Toronto linguistics expert pegged as belonging to the upper-middle class in Yorkshire, England, a lot of attention was paid to him by the British news networks. The *Toronto Sun* published numerous articles on the still unknown assault victim, and the plethora of publicity produced some good and not so good results for Philip. First, an Ontario couple concerned for the plight of the young man opened their home to him. Until that time he'd been staying in a homeless shelter, so living with this family for about two months was a step up from that experience. Neither did he appear to be wanted for any heinous crime. Still, it seemed beyond strange that this young man, who for all outward appearances seemed to be well kempt, well educated and well spoken, didn't have anyone, anywhere, looking for his whereabouts!

The negative outcome of the publicity was that the notoriety was getting to Philip. Because his plight and photo had been widely circulated, he couldn't walk down the street without being confronted by strangers. By June 2001, Philip had long since left the kind family who'd offered him a roof over his head, and he had moved around considerably. He finally settled for a time in Vancouver, where he lived penniless on the streets and lobbied for immigration authorities to help him obtain a passport so that he could turn to the place he came to believe he'd hailed from—England. Of course, to obtain a passport, a person must have a birth certificate, and because Philip still had no memory of who he was, that wasn't possible. He remained in Canada, and without identification, he also remain unemployed.

Somewhere between June 2001 and January 2002, things started to get a little more complicated for Philip. Apparently, an editor of a British gay-porn magazine recognized the photo of Philip as that of one of his models—a 27-year-old Frenchman named Georges Lechit. The only problem was that the real Georges Lechit was eventually located, and he reported that his French passport had been stolen in August 1998.

A lawyer offered his services to the destitute young man on a pro bono basis, but shortly afterwards, Philip's fiancée, Nathalie Herve-Azevedo, and the lawyer received the disturbing news of the British editor's claims, and he quit the case.

Nathalie, however, stood by her man and married Philip in July. A few months later, in October, Philip changed his name to Keith Ryan, and in early 2002 he changed it again, this time to Sywald Skeid. The couple then made their way across the country and set up house in Halifax.

In October 2004, after missing several immigration hearings, Sywald Skeid somehow made an appearance back at the immigration office in Victoria. At that point, Philip, Keith, Sywald, or whatever name he was using, seems to drop off the map.

In May 2005 a man matching Mr. Nobody's description was discovered wandering along England's Kent Beach on the Isle of Sheppey. He was unable to speak and couldn't communicate who he was, and for a time was under the care of a social worker. It was thought that Sywald's wife was in Portugal trying to get a visa there for her husband. He had already been denied a visa in Canada and Britain.

Since that last report, no further suspected sightings of Philip Staufen, a.k.a. Sywald Skeid, have been confirmed. Was his entire story an elaborate hoax? You would hardly think so, given that the entire episode has brought him little more than years of misery and uncertainty. Either way, the mystery of Mr. Nobody's identity will likely remain just that, a mystery. ❧

MIXING BUSINESS WITH PLEASURE

Which among us hasn't taken the opportunity of a business trip to do a little personal shopping and sightseeing? As long as all the work drawing you to a particular location is taken care of, a little R&R never hurt anybody. So when a Lethbridge city councillor attending to community business in Great Falls, Montana, squeezed in a little free time in between meetings, a quick shopping trip was definitely in order. She wanted to find a few small gifts for her three youngsters back home, and who could visit Great Falls without checking out at least some of the area's many attractions?

So on the morning of Saturday, May 3, 2003, before she was to head back to Alberta, 39-year-old Dar Heatherington decided to purchase a cheap, $10 lady's mountain bike at a local pawn shop so that she could spend the morning biking around the city and its many parks and trails. Having already called to let her husband Dave know she'd be late arriving home that night, Dar took a leisurely bike ride, a perfect way to release the many stresses of public office and unwind a bit. Her decision to hang back a while meant she'd miss her daughter's piano recital, but as any good family therapist would say, a little personal time is important for busy mothers.

Meanwhile, life at home in Lethbridge continued on as usual. Dave tidied the house in preparation for his wife's return and gave the kids an early dinner so there'd be no rushing before the piano concert. But as the evening wore on, and he tucked the kids into bed for the night, Dar had still not come home. Dave began to worry. When by midnight she hadn't made it home, he called the police and reported her missing. The only problem was, no one knew if she'd disappeared in Great Falls or somewhere closer to home.

That question was answered relatively quickly when the car she had rented was discovered abandoned in a Great Falls parking lot. Although it wasn't entirely beyond the realm of possibility that she'd intended to leave her car there, it was hard to imagine that the normally well-organized city official would have left her purse and keys as well. Because these items were recovered from the car, it seemed clear that the site was her point last seen. The find caused everyone involved to be worried. Foul play couldn't be ruled out.

While an entourage of investigators—police officers, Great Falls detectives, Lethbridge RCMP, assorted officials from the Cascade County sheriff's office and even a helicopter—had been dispatched in the frantic search for any clue as to Dar's whereabouts, her children and husband were praying and working hard to think good thoughts. With each passing day, tensions rose, and though four days had passed since Dave had last spoken with his wife, he was determined to keep his children thinking positively. "They're making Mother's Day crafts, and they want to give these to their mom on Sunday," he said to *Calgary Sun* reporters.

But things just weren't adding up on the investigative front. While officials remained tight-lipped about the details, they cautiously told various news agencies that they had to examine every possibility, including the idea that the Lethbridge woman chose to vanish. However, a little more digging revealed that Dar had reported to the Lethbridge police that someone had been stalking her for more than a year. Could this individual have followed her to Montana and abducted her there?

On May 8, day five of the case, police got the break they were looking for. It appeared that the Treasure Island Resort in Las Vegas had a distraught woman on their hands. She'd been discovered wandering about the hotel in a daze and was taken to University Medical Center for medical attention. It was Dar, safe and sound. But how did she end up in Las Vegas with no purse, no money, no car? And did her subsequent allegations of being abducted, drugged and possibly sexually assaulted have any merit?

Apparently they didn't. The next day Cascade County attorney Brant Light told CBC news reporters that Dar "admitted she had driven voluntarily from Great Falls to Las Vegas with a man she had met." Later Dar would suggest her comment was a lie to get police to stop interrogating her. David stood by his wife, saying repeatedly that he had seen the bruises inflicted on her body.

At a press conference on June 16, 2003, Dar explained to reporters her version of what had happened. She stated that while riding the bike she'd purchased, the chain fell off. A man stopped, said he could fix the problem and offered her some of his drink, which she accepted. She then started feeling ill and asked the man to help her back to her car. It was at that point that he abducted her.

According to Dar, the man injected her with some type of drug and assaulted her on at least four separate occasions, holding her against her will and making her "do things that were very disturbing." When asked why she had refused medical help from the hospital, she said it was because the doctor and nurse scheduled to examine her were both men. Blood tests taken in Las Vegas didn't reveal any drugs in her system, but Dar stated that her own doctor discovered "traces of barbiturates, opiates and tricyclics."

She went on to explain after extensive interrogation, which she "wouldn't wish on [her] worst enemy," that she had recanted her original statement and began "telling them what they wanted to hear." She said police were "outrageously unjust, undemocratic and disgusting" in their treatment of her, and that she wasn't guilty of the charges of mischief she was now facing in both countries.

In a Montana courtroom, Dar pleaded not guilty to the charges filed against her. In exchange for staying out of trouble for a year and obtaining regular psychiatric counseling, she avoided having a U.S. criminal record. In a Lethbridge court, Dar was convicted on a charge of mischief on June 29, 2004.

She received a 20-month conditional sentence, which included eight months of house arrest and a drug and alcohol abstinence order. The decision was later appealed, and although not reversed, her sentence was reduced to one year. In July 2005, both Dar and her husband were forced to declare bankruptcy, citing legal costs as their biggest financial strain.

Was Dar the unfortunate victim of a brutal assault as she claimed? Is it possible that she'd been harassed and mistreated by law enforcement officials as she'd claimed? Or was she guilty as charged of making the whole thing up? If so, what's the real story behind her Las Vegas excursion? As with most of the cases in this section, the public may never know the rest of the story.

Chapter Ten

When Missing Happens in Multiples

For those of us who haven't been touched by the disappearance of a loved one, just how someone vanishes seemingly into thin air seems incomprehensible. To discover that sometimes two or more persons go missing at one time is simply beyond belief. What follows are Canadian cases documenting people who went missing in multiples of two or more. ∾

LOVEABLE ECCENTRICS

In the community where I live, there's a youngish senior gent who's spent his life, for as long as anyone in these parts can remember, on his bicycle. Every day, even in subzero blizzard conditions, he bikes through town, picks up pop cans and bottles he finds and returns them to the recycling depot for cash. He's a tad grimy, his year-round home is a trailer, and in summer and winter he more or less dresses in the same worn, dirt-caked coat and baggy workpants. Although he lives an impoverished lifestyle, folks around here often joke that he's probably fooled us all and has a well-padded bank account. Still, everyone watches out for him. The lady at the all-you-can-eat Chinese buffet on Main Street always makes sure he gets a few cups of warm coffee. Workers at the bottle depot wait for his daily deposit. And most people smile and wave as he rides by. If a day or two passed without this man's presence, it would be noticed. If his absence was prolonged, our local RCMP detachment would no doubt hear of it and start checking things out.

Such was the case in 1998 when Joan Dorothy Lawrence, affectionately known as the "Cat Lady" of Huntsville, Ontario, went missing.

Not much is known about the early life of 77-year-old Joan. One report speculated she may have been a typesetter or freelance writer in her younger days, but for the last 30 or so years she'd lived in and around Huntsville and became a local legend of sorts. Residents recalled the petite senior who often wrapped a scarf around her long salt-and-pepper hair frequently hitchhiking home, or if she was carrying a couple of bags of groceries, walking ahead to drop one bag and backtracking for the second. She was unkempt, sure, but most folks didn't mind offering her a lift if they happened by.

Joan earned her moniker as the Cat Lady because of her love of cats—and her habit of collecting strays on which to lavish her attention and care. In her last known residence, which was a small garden shack located on Walter Laan's home property and rented to her for the exorbitant rate of $750 a month, Joan was thought to have kept as many as 30 cats. And although she may not have had a lot of money left over from her old-age security and pension cheques for her own sustenance, she always made sure her cats had food. She was sweet and endearing, and when she wasn't spotted around town for a few days, people noticed.

In November 1998 Joan was officially reported missing, and police immediately checked her home and questioned the Laan family. It appeared the Laan siblings—Katherine Eisert, and Paul and Walter Laan—also owned and operated a number of Christian seniors' residences in two rural locations around Huntsville, and after a bit of probing, police learned that three other seniors, John Crofts (70), John Semple (89) and Ralph Grant (69), were also nowhere to be found. The plot, as they say in the movies, was thickening.

As a youngster, John Crofts was tall, dark and dashing. He looked as though nothing would be too difficult for him to accomplish. Born into a loving family, he certainly had all the support he needed to succeed in life. But at the age of 16, John started having difficulties coping and was eventually diagnosed with manic depression (bipolar disorder). Although he had an extended family who loved him and tried to help wherever they could, over the next several decades there were times when he just had to strike out on his own, and ties with his family were severed for a time as he moved from one seedy, downtown Toronto hotel to a homeless shelter and then back again.

In March 1997, Crofts' sister Barb Anderson helped him onto a bus in Peterborough. Anxious to once again strike out on his own, he was destined for Toronto. It was the last Barb saw or heard from him. And then in 2001, police called Barb, asking if she was John Crofts' sister. They explained how he'd been living at a homeless shelter when he was approached with the offer of a room in one of the Laans' retirement homes. Crofts took up the offer but hasn't been seen since 1998. Sad news though it was, contacting Barb gave police something to work with in their investigation. They could perhaps learn a little more about the missing man himself, now that they knew for certain he hadn't left the retirement home to return to his family.

Ties to the pasts of Ralph Grant and John Semple would be a little harder to figure out. From what police could learn, Grant was thought to hail from Stewiacke, Nova Scotia, and Semple from Ulster, Northern Ireland. Grant often went by the nickname of "Duke," and given that his lower jaw had been surgically removed because of cancer, police had an easily distinguishable physical feature to go on. Semple, the oldest of the three men, was little more than a blank slate—173 centimetres (5 feet 8 inches) in height and a lean 68 kilograms (150 pounds), according to his missing person's poster. Old-age retirement homes, homeless shelters, hospitals, hotels, bank accounts— every available avenue was checked to determine what could have become of these individuals, but investigators could only discover that the trail leading away from the Laan's retirement home was stone cold.

Other things were clear, though. All three men resided at the Laan's retirement home on Yearly Road in Huntsville. All three men, as well as Joan Lawrence, went missing between January 1998 and January 1999. And no member of the Laan family, who all had a vested interest in the four seniors, ever reported any of these seniors as missing to the police or RCMP. Yet the old-age security cheques for Semple, Grant and Crofts were still coming in and being cashed, along with cheques belonging to several other residents who had once resided at the home and since passed away. One news report pegged the alleged theft of social security and pension money to be as much as $120,000.

Furthermore, it appeared that the Laans were scouting elderly, fragile-looking seniors with little or no family connections; they visited homeless shelters such as Toronto's Seaton House looking for men. On at least one occasion they publicized their affordable, Christian retirement home, with promises of many activities and a loving environment. Those assurances were why Crofts and Grant moved to Huntsville, only to find their new digs little more than an "unregulated rooming house" and far from the kind of Christian environment they were expecting.

Police and RCMP quickly realized they now had a two-track investigation going on: the case of four missing seniors and an embezzlement investigation with vulnerable seniors as the victims. In 2003 and 2004, three Laan siblings, Katherine, Walter and Paul, "were convicted of embezzling money from seniors" and using the cash to pad their own bank accounts. They were each given conditional sentences.

But the story was far from over. On Friday, October 14, 2005, Walter Laan pleaded guilty to a string of violent home invasions in Rockwood, Muskoka, the Durham Region and Brantford, robbing and often beating the elderly residents who lived there. He received a 13-year sentence and is currently serving his time in Fenbrook. Since his bout with the law, Paul Laan has completed a course of religious studies at a Seventh Day Adventist college in Lacombe, Alberta, and was last known to be working as a missionary in Korea. Katherine was found to be teaching at a Christian school in Barrie early in 2006. On learning of her involvement in the Huntsville case after an airing of a *W-FIVE* documentary entitled "Mystery of Muskoka," the school was closed.

Meanwhile, what of the four missing seniors, who are all listed on the Ontario Provincial Police's Resolve website? Is it possible, living in a land of lakes and wilderness, that they simply wandered off and became lost and disoriented? Could they have died of natural causes and no one notified of their deaths?

"We're treating this as a homicide investigation," Detective Inspector Dave Quigley said to *W-FIVE*. "This is not a cold case, it is an active investigation that's been consistently investigated since it started in November of 1998…we have a duty to look out for people like this because they are so vulnerable... society has to look out for people like this, people who can't protect themselves."

Rewards of $50,000 have been offered by OPP for information leading to the solving of this mystery in all four cases. ∾

BOYHOOD BUDDIES

Young boys aged 14 and 15 are just beginning to bridge the gap between adolescence and adulthood. They're growing long and gangly and having to learn how to adjust to their bodies all over again. They might be sprouting some facial hair, here and there. And girls aren't quite as disgusting as they once appeared. Still, teenagers are as full of energy and mischief as ever, and parents of youngsters in this age group might find themselves wishing they could bottle some of that energy and use it to replenish their own. Fifteen-year-old John McCormick and his 14-year-old buddy (Lloyd) Eric Larsfolk were just such a pair.

Eric and his family originally lived in Fort Erie, located at the eastern tip of the Great Lake that bears the same name and just a stone's throw from the state of New York. The Larsfolks lived in a land rich in heritage—the War of 1812 was partly fought in this and the surrounding areas, and Fort Erie was a stop on the Underground Railway. As far as recreation goes, Fort Erie is rich in walking trails, beaches and, of course, Niagara Falls isn't far away, so there is no shortage of things to do.

The Larsfolks lived and worked in the region for most of Eric's young life, enjoying the natural beauty surrounding them and contributing to it with the bounty produced at the family's greenhouse venture. Over time, however, the business started to fail. By the summer of 1981 the family had lost their much-loved greenhouse and, anxious for a new start, moved to the Caledon area just north of Richmond Hill and a short drive from Lake Ontario.

The town of Caledon was officially formed in 1974, and according to the 2006 census, boasts a population of slightly more than 57,000—about twice the population of Fort Erie. There are no less than 70 parks totalling 300 acres in the community, including plenty of hiking and biking trails. Located in the Regional Municipality of Peel, which is technically in the Greater Toronto Area, the surrounding countryside has maintained its rural charm, and the Larsfolks happily found themselves a farmhouse on a piece of heaven they could call their own.

Although the McCormick family lived on the next property, on a sprawling 150-acre farm, they were next-door neighbours by rural standards. Their young son John had just spent several weeks visiting relatives in Virginia and didn't get to meet his new young neighbour until mid-August 1981, but Eric and John hit it off immediately. Both boys had an abundance of energy that only a lot of activity would quench, and the two spent many hours riding their bikes or digging up the back field in an old Chevy truck John used to hone his driving skills for that long-awaited day when he was old enough to get his driver's licence. So when Eric told his parents, Lloyd and Beverley, that he was heading over to John's house after dinner on August 24, they weren't concerned. It had been a particularly exciting day—Eric had just won a new bicycle at the Dairy Queen in town, and the family had gone down to pick it up and proudly snap a few pictures of their son in the front of the burger joint. It's a photograph they'd hold dear for the rest of their lives—the last picture ever taken of their young son.

At about 11:00 that same night, the Larsfolks were startled by a pounding on their front door. They opened it to find John's mother Joyce in a frantic state. She'd been out for the evening and wasn't aware the two boys were supposedly at her house, because aside from Eric's bike propped outside the house, the boys were nowhere to be seen. She was concerned, and she had every right to be. Just a few weeks earlier, her husband John Sr. had beaten their son so badly that he had to be hospitalized. The event was what had precipitated John Jr.'s trip to his Virginia relatives.

Before long, a massive search was launched. John Sr., an alcoholic who was more than a little drunk at the time of the boys' disappearance, was questioned immediately, but said he didn't know where the boys were. And though he made an effort to assist the search party that night, it was the only time he did so, and neither he nor his wife made a public appeal for the safe return of their son. The Larsfolks, however, have never stopped searching in the more than 20 years since Eric's disappearance. "We turned the world upside down to find them," Lloyd said in a September 29, 2002 *Toronto Sun* newspaper article. Investigators were able to track the boys' footprints to a gravel pit located on the McCormick property, but the trail went cold at a nearby fence.

Over the years, the McCormick property has been repeatedly searched, ponds dragged, barns, buildings and old wells examined, but no remains of the boys have ever been discovered. At one point the Larsfolks even contacted psychics to assist them in their search for Eric, desperate to get a lead on what happened to their son. The psychics' revelations were hardly comforting—one mentioned that the boys' bodies had been eaten up in a lime pit, while another mentioned a UFO intervention of sorts. Still, Lloyd and Beverley never lost hope.

John McCormick Sr. died of cirrhosis of the liver in 1987. Joyce subsequently sold the farm and moved, trying in the best way she knew to put the horror of the last years behind her. Although the Ontario Provincial Police have never publicly declared a suspect in the case, they have been reported as stating that their prime suspect is "deceased."

For Lloyd Larsfolk, that's a small comfort indeed. If Eric was dead, Lloyd would never know what precipitated such a senseless act that squelched all the promise his son had to offer the world. Beverley died in 2000, never being able to give her son a proper burial. At the very least it's something the Larsfolks desperately wanted to do.

In the meantime, no discovery of his son's body spells the very slightest bit of hope for Lloyd. And although the boys are not expected to be found alive, Eric and John Jr. remain listed as "missing" on the OPP Internet site; Child Find; Canada's federal government webpage, "Our Missing Children"; the Doe Network, and with other agencies. ∾

THE JACK FAMILY

In the summer of 1989, Ronald Jack was a little down on his luck. With the kids on summer break from school, Ronald no doubt would have loved to take his two young boys and wife on vacation. A trip to Disneyland was an unlikely reality for the financially struggling family, but pitching a tent somewhere and spending a few days fishing was certainly something they would enjoy. He could almost taste his wife Doreen's fresh-fried salmon cooked over an open fire. And then, just as quickly as the image materialized, it dissolved, and he was back to his reality and the prospect of finding a new job to provide for his young family. Times were tight back in 1989; jobs weren't as abundant as they would be in the late 1990s and into the first decade of the 21st century, and Ronald was more than just a little concerned about his current employment circumstances.

Then suddenly, when he least expected it, a chance offering of a two-week contract came his way via a new buddy he'd met at a local tavern. Without giving it a second thought, Ronald accepted the job and rushed home to share his good news with his family. Sure it would take the young man away from his Prince George home, but the bright side was that the opportunity included a job for Doreen as well, and their children, nine-year-old Russell and four-year-old Ryan, could accompany them.

It was the middle of the night when they left, but they were anxious to get started. The couple bundled up their young-sters for the journey, packed a few necessities and favourite belongings and left their home on Strathcona Avenue. They headed out on Highway 16 westbound, along the infamous Highway of Tears.

As the young family set out for their new adventure, Ronald thought he'd better not get too far ahead of himself before letting someone in the family know where the foursome were off to. Just outside Prince George, about 50 kilometres down the road, is a favourite roadside stop called Bednesti Cluculz Lake. A small collection of cabins surround the neigh-bouring Bednesti resort's restaurant, lounge, convenience store and gas pumps, and folks passing through Prince George typi-cally like to stop there for a bite to eat and a breath of fresh air before continuing on to Vanderhoof, Burns Lake or points west. The food's always good—homemade versus the fast kind—and the conversation is typically lively. Of course, very little was open when Ronald pulled up to use the pay phone at 1:30 AM on August 2. Still, he could safely park the car off the often-treacherous stretch of highway and near the resort while checking in with his mother.

There was no mistaking the excitement in his voice as he shared his newfound good fortune. He explained how he and the family would be gone for between 10 days and two weeks to work on a ranch or logging camp—it was 1:30 AM after all, and when called upon to remember details, Ronald's mother wasn't sure. She also wasn't clear about where, geographically speaking, the family was headed, but going off to work camps at odd hours and for prolonged periods of time isn't out of the ordinary for folks in BC's northern interior, so Ronald's family wasn't overly concerned.

But when 10 days turned into two weeks, and then two weeks turned into three, and the family still hadn't heard from Ronald or Doreen, they began to worry. The RCMP was notified of the odd disappearance and the Jack family's Strathcona Avenue home was searched. With most of their belongings still in the house, it seemed obvious to investigators that the family had every intention of returning to their Prince George home. But since that late night phone call almost 20 years ago, none of the Jacks' relatives or friends have heard from them.

The case of Ronald, Doreen, Ryan and Russell was the first, and remains, to date, the only disappearance in the country involving an entire family. It was initially thought that the family might have veered off the road, though the suggestion is unlikely. As remote as northern BC can be, loggers, guide outfitters and area residents are in and out of the bush on a regular basis, and no sign of such an occurrence has ever been discovered. Of course, as with any missing person's case, the police have to consider the possibility that the family chose to disappear. RCMP believe this, too, is improbable, as the Jack clan were close-knit and in regular contact. In the minds of everyone who knew them, the thought of the foursome taking off on purpose was the least likely scenario.

That left law enforcement officials with the last, grim option of foul play, which seems to be a greater possibility according to how the historic case is listed on the website of the Prince George RCMP Crime Stoppers. The last confirmed sighting of Ronald Jack had him speaking with a Caucasian male at the First Litre Pub in Prince George. Ronald's mother received his excited phone call later that same night. Could it be possible that a predator sensed Ronald's personal difficulties and took advantage of his desperation? One has to assume the case received at least some publicity, and if the offer of work was legitimate, you would think the purveyor of that offer would have come forward. If indeed a predator lured the Jack family to parts unknown, what would be the reason? What thrill could someone get in terrorizing an innocent young family?

Although the case has long since grown cold, RCMP continue to revisit it from time to time, hoping that sometime in the future the clues needed to solve this mystery, which has tormented those who loved the Jack family, will be uncovered. ❧

The Wrong Crowd?

To those who knew them, Nickolas and Lisa Mo Masee were like any other ambitious couple—hard working, career oriented and very much in love. But when they suddenly disappeared, it wasn't long before their ordinary veneer was exposed as a lot more complicated than it initially seemed.

Beautiful and vibrant, 39-year-old Lisa Mo Masee didn't have any trouble attracting customers to her chair at Yokoi Hair Design on Vancouver's Cambie Street. Her friends and family described her as sweet and outgoing, but sensible and reliable, too. Married to Nickolas Masee, 16 years her senior and a successful businessman, she likely didn't have to work but enjoyed the personal challenge and interaction her career of choice offered her.

Nickolas, a Dutch immigrant who moved to Nova Scotia in 1955, clearly maintained a strong work ethic, climbing up the employment food chain and across the country, from bank teller and all steps in between to the position of executive account manager with the Bank of Montréal in Vancouver. After more than three decades of experience with that company, he opted to retire in early spring of 1994 and try on a couple of different hats, one as a stock promoter for what was called CentrePoint Enterprises, and another as a director for Turbodyne Technologies Inc. Turbodyne's corporate website describes the company as "a leading engineering company in the design and development of patented electrically assisted air-charging technology that enhances the performance of internal combustion engines." Much of the company's history seems to be shrouded in mystery; research and development are only vaguely touched upon, and the one contact number listed is a voice-operated calling system.

And according to a report in Reuters, Turbodyne hasn't made a lot of money yet—one financial summary for the business lists a zero-dollar cash balance, zero-percent revenue growth over one year—no revenue and no profit.

Some sources have also tied Turbodyne to one-time Vancouver promoter Harry Moll. A controversial character, Moll was reported to be involved with a number of public firms on the now-defunct Vancouver Stock Exchange. At least some of his business ventures allegedly resulted in folks losing a lot of money, though Turbodyne doesn't necessarily fit into this category. Nevertheless, Moll was said to dance a fine line between legitimate trading and violating "insider-trading provisions of the Securities Act," at least according to a BC legislative report highlighting the afternoon sitting of May 2, 1988.

Fred Hofman, one of Nickolas' associates, was also a curious character. Hofman had been a member of the First Christian Reformed Church in Vancouver for more than 20 years. *Canadian Christianity* reported in May 2003 that Hofman, an accountant by profession, allegedly took money from parishioners to invest in U.S. treasury bills, promising a hefty profit in return. Eager to take him up on his suggestion—after all, he was a numbers guy—people flocked to him with their investment money.

For some, it may have only represented a small portion of their worth. For others, it was significantly more. Either way, they'd all lost their money in what was considered nothing short of immoral business practice. In March 1989 Hofman was fined $50,000 by the British Columbia Securities Commission and banned from trading for five years for "acting as a portfolio manager without registration." Six lawsuits totalling more than $10 million were filed against the man, and another 61 counts of fraud were laid against him by the RCMP. But by that time, in 1991, Hofman had fled Canada for Australia.

Neither Harry Moll nor Fred Hofman is directly tied to the Masees' disappearance, but the suggestion has been made that some unprofitable business dealings between Nickolas and an unknown investor could have been the impetus for whatever became of the missing couple. The day Nickolas and Lisa disappeared, the couple was spotted at the lounge of the Westin Bayshore. It was August 10, 1994. The witness stated that Nickolas had a worried look on his face. Nickolas fully expected to meet with a potential business associate who had voiced interest in investing $10 million in one of Nickolas' ventures, though there was no clear indication what business venture was being referred to. The investor never showed. That left Nickolas with an uneasy feeling.

Investigative reporter Anna Marie D'Angelo examined the missing persons' case in an article in the *North Shore News* dated October 26, 1998. By then the case had gone cold but was far from forgotten. North Vancouver RCMP investigating the Masees' disappearance had determined it likely that Nickolas and Lisa were abducted from their home and killed shortly thereafter. When the couple was reported missing and their home searched, the house was found unlocked, the garage door open and Nickolas' convertible easily accessible. For a security-conscious man such as Nickolas, the scene screamed something was definitely wrong.

Over the years, speculation on the circumstances surrounding the Masees' disappearance has run the gamut from being the result of a bad business deal, where someone lost a lot of money, to the couple leaving voluntarily, or to their being placed in witness protection and their identities changed. According to the *North Shore News,* however, the official train of thought by North Vancouver RCMP suggested there was definite organized crime involvement in what they have long-since labelled a double homicide, and that "there are a number of people from Nick's professional circle that know what happened to Nick, why it happened and who did it, but they are all afraid."

Chapter Eleven

Mommy, Where Are You?

Back in September 1987 I was expecting my fourth child, any day in fact, and my oldest, Peter, was just starting kindergarten. Walking to the local elementary school, though not all that far from our home, meant crossing a railway track twice a day, and knowing my son's inquisitive mind, I could see him opting for a stroll down the tracks instead of coming straight home from school. With two toddlers at home and me as big as a beached whale, gathering my entourage together for twice daily walks to school and back seemed out of the question. The only other option was to have Peter catch the school bus, which stopped around the corner and was about four blocks away. Every morning I would stand outside and watch until I lost sight of him long before he'd ever made it to the bus stop. Every day I worried, but never more than on the day he didn't come home from school.

Usually he'd bound in the front door by 3:45 in the afternoon, most times with a friend or two in tow. Not that day. That evening, I waited and waited. By the time his father came home around 5:00 PM, I was frantic. I left my husband with the toddlers and toured the neighbourhood by car. At the time, our family was living in a low-income neighbourhood made up of almost 100 townhouses with a wild and well-earned reputation. That only increased my worry. An hour or two went by, and still no Peter. In between vision blurred by tears and a throat hoarse with fear, I started wondering at what point I should call in the police. Nearly defeated, I decided to widen my search again, this time moving down the block a bit more before I turned back for home and dialed 911. That's when something caught my eye. Just for a second I thought I saw two young boys going into a townhouse. One of the boys looked like Peter, but I wasn't sure. It was nearing 7:00 PM, the streets had been pretty much empty for some time, and I drove by to be sure my son hadn't entered a stranger's house. He had.

I was never so equally relieved and angry in my life. To me it was unforgivable that another boy's caregiver would allow my child carte blanche to enter her house and stay these several hours without even a phone call home. As for Peter, what was he thinking? Hadn't I drilled it through that beautiful but stubborn brain of his that he must never go with a stranger?

The entire experience had shaken me to the core. While Peter's dad may have thought I'd overreacted, I knew we were lucky. Peter was coming home. Nothing bad had happened.

And I had another chance to reinforce the stranger rule. Hopefully, next time he'd remember. Hopefully, he'd never have to. ∾

HERE AND GONE

Six-year-old Tania Marie Murrell was a big girl now. She'd been attending grade one at Edmonton's Grovner Elementary School for four months, and she just loved it—you could tell by the bounce in her step as she headed to school each morning. With saucer-shaped brown eyes, a mop of sandy brown hair tamed by two braids and an ear-to-ear smile that would melt Scrooge himself, Tania was a sweetheart.

The youngster's daily routine, at lunch and after school, was to meet her five-year-old brother John once the bell rang, and the two would walk home together. For some reason, just before noon on Thursday, January 20, 1983, Tania didn't wait for her brother. John made it home safely for lunch that day, but she was never seen again.

Tania's disappearance precipitated what was to that point the largest door-to-door search in Alberta's capital. Money poured in, and a reward of $40,000 for information on her whereabouts was established. Tania's parents were convinced she'd been abducted, since not a trace of her or her belongings was ever found. And according to Detective John McLeod, one of the investigators interviewed by the *Edmonton Journal* at the time, it wasn't a stretch to think the child was taken forcibly. Children at this age might typically react by doing what they're told instead of screaming and running away. Once abducted, Tania then could have been convinced that her parents didn't want her anymore.

The Murrells had another reason for thinking someone took Tania. The family suspected an old acquaintance was responsible. But those suspicions, along with tips pointing to the Cooking Lake area, either weren't followed up on or didn't produce any solid leads, and the whole experience was destroying the Murrell family. At first, the situation initiated some positive action. Tania's mother, Vivian; father, Jack; and a network of friends and concerned citizens established the Tania Murrell Missing Children Society, Canada's first not-for-profit organization focused on missing children. Tania's disappearance also prompted a concerned Calgary woman to form the Canadian version of America's Child Find.

In the midst of continuing their search for Tania, Vivian and Jack tried to live as normal a life as possible. Two years after Tania's disappearance, daughter Elysia was born. The couple moved their young family to Kelowna in an effort to start over again. But it wasn't long before the strain of the experience took its toll, and in time, Vivian and Jack split up. Eventually Elysia moved with her father to Ontario, where she continues to live today. Jack has since passed away, never knowing what became of his little girl. But Vivian, who still lives in Kelowna, continues to hope Tania is alive, as does Elysia, the sister Tania never met.

Tears still flow freely for Vivian whenever she thinks about the bright-eyed baby girl who'd be 30 by now and likely have children of her own. The pain doesn't subside, and until a body is discovered, both Vivian and Elysia will continue to publicize Tania's abduction in the hope that the person or persons responsible for her disappearance will suffer from a stroke of conscience and call the police. And if Tania is out there, somewhere, she may learn of their search and call home. ∞

PLAYGROUND PANIC

March 24, 1991, was a beautiful sunny Sunday. The warmth of the sun cut through the last chill of winter, reinforcing the hope that after a long and dreary cool season, spring was finally here to stay. At this time of year it's not unusual to see a few Brant geese flying overhead on their way to their summer roost. And although it was still early in the season, it wasn't a huge stretch to see a MacGillivray or any other warbler variety starting to appear on the scene.

Despite the fact that Victoria doesn't suffer from anything remotely close to the long, cold winters of the Prairies, by the time the calendar says spring is here, folks are more than a little eager to get out of doors again. This particular Sunday was no exception. Couples were pushing strollers along park walkways, toddlers were testing out playgrounds, and just imagining the supper burgers sizzling on the barbie was enough to make anyone's mouth water.

For Crystal and Bruce Dunahee and their two children, four-year-old Michael and 16-month-old Caitlin, the day promised fresh air, exercise and family time. Crystal was participating in a softball tournament near what was then the Blanchard Elementary School (now University Canada West). Bruce would be cheering her on, along with Caitlin, while Michael wanted to try out the equipment at the school's playground. With Bruce and Caitlin just metres away, Michael was allowed to play, with the admonishment that he not leave the area or wander off with any of the other children.

Caring for young children is never a stationary experience, and not five minutes into the game, Bruce was up checking to make sure Michael had remained where he promised. What Bruce discovered would precipitate nothing short of pandemonium in the lives of the Dunahee family and propel them into the media spotlight in a way they've never totally escaped— Michael was nowhere to be found. The playground was empty. A dark, foreboding fear must have clenched Bruce, and then Crystal, as they searched for Michael. Police were called immediately to the scene, and the massive search that followed remains one of the largest in Canadian history. Family members were checked thoroughly, friends queried; in fact, anyone who'd had any involvement in the Dunahees' lives was approached, but nothing came of this line of questioning.

Despite how statistics point to the rarity of the situation, it was beginning to look as if Michael had been the victim of a stranger abduction. If so, the abductor hadn't left a trace of evidence. And when the ground search didn't yield a single solid clue, it was eventually called off. Other than Michael's parents and one other couple, no one seemed to have noticed the young lad with the hint of red in his hair and a scattering of freckles on his nose.

During the first while, the Dunahee tragedy garnered ink in papers across the continent. Tips poured into police head-quarters by an endless stream of well-meaning people whose hearts ached for the family. Today, 16 years later, detectives continue their examination into Michael's disappearance. Crystal became involved with Child Find British Columbia and was a strong voice in support of the implementation of the Amber Alert system in that province—a mass media messaging system that pumps out information about missing youth. The family is also involved in the annual Michael Dunahee "Keep the Hope Alive" Fun Run, which raises money for Child Find initiatives. The Dunahees continued producing posters with age-enhanced photographs updating what Michael would look like today and distributing them anywhere they can. And, of course, they keep looking and hoping—Crystal has told reporters that she believes that Michael is still alive, waiting to come home.

On March 24, 2006, the 15th anniversary of his disap-pearance, the reward leading to information on Michael Duna-hee's whereabouts was raised to $100,000, bringing with it a deluge of new tips to add to the more than 11,000 already collected by police. In one instance, a young man living in the BC Interior was thought to look just like one of the age-enhanced images of Michael, but DNA ruled out that possibility. Another call came in from a Victoria resident who on touring Kentucky said she'd seen a photograph of a young man matching the age-enhanced image on Michael's missing person's poster. That, too, fell through. But police remain hopeful, saying tips of Michael sightings continue to come in. They are also following up on other new leads. Hopefully, the heart and effort of everyone involved will, in time, pay off. ∾

HOW SAFE IS HOME?

For most youngsters, the beginning of July signifies a long stretch of splashing through outdoor sprinklers on dusty, hot days, shooting hoops in the neighbour's driveway and playing endless games of street hockey. Libraries across the country host day camps for kids of all ages looking for something to do, as are churches and boys and girls clubs. And who could forget about the Dickie-Dee ice cream vendors touring city neighbourhoods in an effort to separate kids from their coins. Nothing spells fun like summer, and the youngsters who made up the Keepness family were looking forward to the next two months of freedom.

On the evening of Monday, July 5, 2004, the Keepness youngsters were snuggled together in the family's Regina living room, taking in the movie *The Gladiator* with their mother Lorena and her boyfriend, Dean McArthur. Sometime around

8:30 PM, Lorena and Dean had an argument, and Dean left. He bumped into Russell Sheepskin, his buddy who was also a boarder in the Keepness home, and the two decided to head to the local bar for a few drinks. Once the movie was over, Lorena and the kids continued to channel surf, and the night ended around 11:00 PM after an episode of the *Simpsons*.

"They were kinda dragging around, you know, stalling, stalling to go to bed. And finally I said 'OK guys, bedtime, gimme kiss.' And I kissed them all, and they went trailing upstairs," Lorena told CBC reporters. Five-year-old Tamra followed her 10-year-old brother Raine and another sibling to the upstairs bedroom while her 11-year-old sister, Summer, and sister Tannis stayed downstairs. As the oldest of the children, Summer took over as caregiver while Lorena went to visit a friend who lived about a block away. Lorena told Summer to lock the front door as she left and not to open it for anyone. She'd call as soon as she got to her friend's house and give Summer the phone number should she need her mother to come back home. Lorena called Summer with that number at about midnight.

While mom was out having a few drinks with friends down the road, there seemed to be a fair amount of traffic in and around the Keepness home. Sometime that night, Russell said he entered the Keepness residence and, seeing through the eyes of someone who'd had a few too many, seemed to remember making himself a spaghetti dinner—other sources have him blacking out and later waking in his downstairs bedroom. He also said he remembered seeing the children sleeping in the living room, and in one report said Tamra was also on the couch. Meanwhile, Dean returned home, also in a drunken stupor, and got into a physical altercation with Russell. Dean threatened to bring back a couple of his buddies to finish Russell off and left through the front door. Russell decided not to wait around to see if Dean would make good on his threat and took off out the back door, eventually making his way to the hospital for stitches. It was around 3:00 AM. Neither man remembered locking the front door.

Dean would later face charges for assault causing bodily harm as a result of the altercation, but as he left the Keepness home for a second time that night, he appeared to have forgotten his immediate threat to recruit a few buddies to finish Russell off. At that moment, his main concern was to find a place to sleep for the night, since he and Lorena were still at odds, and he decided to go to his aunt's. Admitting he was intoxicated and adding that his aunt had just moved, he wandered neighbourhood streets trying to orient himself. He estimated that it took him until about 5:30 in the morning before he finally found her home.

Sometime after 3:00 AM Lorena also returned home. She too admitted to being intoxicated and, since she believed the front door was locked, had to crawl through a window to get into the house. Although it was all a bit of a blur, she reported seeing two of her children, Summer and Tannis, sleeping in the living room just as she'd left them earlier the night before. Lorena decided to sleep on the unoccupied couch, and that's where she awoke a few hours later when her mother, Lois Shepherd, arrived around 9:00 AM. When asked, Lois recalled the front door was open.

Summer and her brother Raine were eager to get on with their day and before long ran out the door and made their way to a day camp that was being hosted by the local community centre. With the exception of Tamra, the other Keepness youngsters had already finished breakfast when Lorena asked one of them to go upstairs and wake their baby sister. That's when the family discovered the five-year-old was missing.

The little girl with the bobbed haircut, playful smile and glint in her eye fairly radiates her name—Tamra Jewel. Bright as a shiny new gemstone, her personality almost leaps off the pages of the missing person's poster bearing her photograph and name. Her mysterious disappearance not only launched one of the biggest searches in Regina's history, but it also struck fear in the hearts of parents everywhere. The situation felt a little like déjà vu, bringing to mind Elizabeth Smart's middle-of-the-night abduction from the bedroom of her Salt Lake City home in June 2002. How can such a thing happen—and in our own backyard? This is Canada, after all. Are we no longer safe in our own homes?

As family, friends, neighbours and associates of the Keepness family were being questioned, police officers and search and rescue volunteers continued to scrutinize alleyways, buildings and dumpsters in a nine-block area surrounding the family home in an effort to find some trace of the missing girl. In time, the search was expanded to include "more than 100 city blocks just east of the downtown core." Following up on tips received, including Aboriginal visions on Tamra's whereabouts, police eventually searched the wooded sections surrounding Regina, along with the waters of the nearby Wascana Creek. Still, nothing even remotely tied to the missing girl was uncovered.

After a week of searching, representing more than 5000 hours, police called off the search for the missing youngster. But the little girl had captured the heart of a city, and police officers who'd put their heart and soul into the case weren't about to give up. The investigation continued, and Regina police chief Cal Johnston told reporters, "We will find Tamra. And if there has been criminal conduct, we will find those involved."

While the police began re-interviewing Tamra's family, along with a list of five people Lorena suggested could be responsible for her daughter's disappearance, members of Saskatchewan's First Nations community were gathering to continue their own unofficial search. Focusing on new tips, police would from time to time organize other searches in new, previously unexamined locations, which included a First Nations reserve. And Tamra's plight would receive international attention as her photograph and particulars were posted on *America's Most Wanted* website on July 16. Her story was aired on July 23.

Today, the mystery behind Tamra's disappearance remains unsolved, but police continue to actively investigate. A cash reward of $25,000 for information on Tamra's whereabouts was authorized by the Regina Board of Police Commissioners on July 13, 2004, and remains in effect. In April 2006, a six-person task force looking into the case was reduced to two. But any new information continues to be followed up. ∽

NEVER SAY GOODBYE

When asked to describe the measure of a mother's love, it's easy to come up with several adjectives—everlasting, unconditional, pure, steadfast...the list goes on. But perhaps the depth of such a love is never more clearly measured than when a child goes missing. Although the two cases that follow are from the 1950s, they remain posted on the Doe Network. And if an Internet entry on the *Unsolved Mysteries* website is any indication, at least one of the mothers involved was still alive and wondering about her son as recently as 2001.

The first story begins with Clifford Edward Sherwood and his pal, Georges Grumbley, heading off to school on the morning of October 21, 1954. The weather's a bit crisp in Verdun, Québec, at this time of the year, but that wouldn't prevent two nine-year-old lads from dallying along the path, kicking up fallen leaves as they walked and discussing what they wanted from Santa for Christmas. Neither youngster would ever experience the thrill of Christmas morning—at least, not in the way they were expecting to. Both disappeared on their way to school that day, and no trace of the boys has ever been discovered. The only clue to Clifford's well-being was a strange phone call he'd made to his aunt the next day. She is documented as remembering him saying, "Auntie, Auntie Hilda." And then nothing but a dial tone.

There is virtually no further information about young Georges. Clifford, however, did have a family history that raised some flags. His parents were separated, and while his four sisters were residing with his father in the Vancouver area, the young boy remained with his mother in Verdun. The separation must have been far from an amicable one, because Clifford's now-deceased father was long suspected of having abducted Clifford. Still, nothing concrete was established, and the senior Sherwood died in April 1976 without ever being charged in connection with the case.

The notice posted on the *Unsolved Mysteries* website seems to suggest the possibility that Clifford is still alive. It supports the suggestion with photographs of the father with a much older-looking Clifford, and the boy's mother and sisters once thought they'd traced him through his driving records. But then the suspected lead didn't pan out after the individual moved without leaving a forwarding address. On this site, after each missing person's entry, the individual submitting the search request is asked to answer the question of why they are posting a message. In this case the writer simply says, "I am trying to end a grieving mother's pain of almost 50 years without her son."

~

Grief over a missing son began for a Calgary mother on Christmas Eve 1957. Despite it being the day before Christmas, Madeline Nelson had to punch in at work. Typically, her neighbour at the Inglewood Auto Court babysat her three-year-old son Larry, but that day she was unavailable and referred a worried Madeline to her sister-in-law.

Details on exactly what happened to little Larry are sketchy, but when Madeline returned home from work that day he had vanished. Calgary City Police thought the toddler may have wandered near a group of children playing by the Bow River and fallen through the thin ice. With that in mind, they dragged the river but recovered nothing. For Madeline, however, the likelihood of Larry wandering near the river was next to nonexistent, because he was afraid of water. That fact, along with the absence of a body, must have fired the young mother's hope for years to come, as the prime suspect in her mind was none other than the boy's father, Edward Sawchuk. Madeline reported that he had tried to abduct Larry once before, and she wouldn't put it past him to try it again.

She would never find out if she was right, at least not through a confession by Edward. On June 24, 1975, he committed suicide in the Saskatchewan River. To date, no trace of Larry has ever turned up. As with the case of Clifford Sherwood, relatives continue to hope for new leads to surface and placed a request for information on his whereabouts on the Internet site Cyber Pages International Inc., dedicated to people who are looking for lost and missing relatives. ॐ

Just the Facts

In a report penned in 2005 by National Missing Children Services, the National Police Services, and RCMP, no less than 66,548 children went missing that year in this country. Of those, 51,280 were listed as runaways; 12,079 vanished for unknown reasons; 2062 for other reasons (children reported missing by a detention home or other similar institution); 704 wandered off in any number of circumstances, such as from a campsite or social service care; 349 were abducted by a parent; 30 were kidnapped; and 45 went missing by accident.

A missing child is traumatic regardless the reason, but perhaps one of the most difficult statistics law enforcement has to deal with is the 12,079 children who go missing for completely unknown reasons. Children who fall into this category leave investigators with little to work with. Most of the cases listed in this chapter fall into that category. Here are a few more 2005 statistics on missing children in Canada:

- 78 percent of all missing children were runaways. Of that number, 57 percent (38,041) were females and 43 percent (28,507) were males.

- Of the 30 reported kidnappings, 21 were of females and nine of males.

- Parental abductions of males and females were fairly equally divided, with 173 females to 176 males.

- Drug or alcohol dependency was cited as a factor in 23 percent of these cases.

- The point last seen for the children reported missing in 2005 can be divided as follows:

  - 32 percent went missing from home;

  - 14 percent went missing from child care;

  - 21 percent went missing from foster care;

  - 26 percent went missing from some type of institution, including school; and

  - Less than one percent vanished from a shopping centre, workplace or while on vacation.

Most of us can remember our parents telling us at least once during our childhood not to talk to strangers. It's still a valid admonishment, but today there's so much more youngsters need to know. Oftentimes a child goes missing with someone they trust, maybe even a parent.

Organizations such as Child Find Canada, and the National Centre for Missing and Exploited Children, maintain checklists on the best ways to protect your child from a possible abduction in all types of situations and provide information on what to do if your child goes missing.

Chapter Twelve

Missing by Choice

Marla is a 35-year-old single career gal who's making her way up the corporate ladder. She's a driven, Type-A personality, showing up at work long before anyone else and the last to turn off the computer at night. Her work is flawless, so much so that whenever a job needs doing, Marla's the gal who's commandeered. In short, she's the perfect employee.

For those under her command, she's also a demanding boss. There are times when Marla can come across as harsh and unreasonable, and those reporting to her find her a bit of a tyrant. If asked, the thought that Marla had a soft spot is not something most who know her would acknowledge. At the very least it wouldn't be considered a weakness in her veneer. She's Ms. Professional, all the way. No nonsense about Marla.

Her aura of perfection doesn't stop in the workplace, either. To Marla's friends, she's a rock, someone they can always turn to for a shoulder to cry on. To her lover she's even a bit of a tiger, wildly passionate and demanding. To her mother, Marla is everything one could hope for in a daughter. However, what no one knows is that under the mask Marla wears in public, she is a vulnerable, somewhat overwhelmed young woman who's terrified of failing and feels far less secure in her abilities than others might think. So when she doesn't show up for work one day and hasn't contacted family, friends or colleagues, everyone fears the worst. Something terrible must have happened to Marla. But there might be another explanation.

There are times when we all feel far less capable than others might peg us to be. Regardless what our colleagues and boss might say about the positive quality of our work, we feel sadly lacking. Our personal trainer might warn us against losing any more weight, but we feel there's at least another five extra pounds to lose—even after we'd lost the five pounds we spotted last month. We feel as if we fail our friends. We think we've disappointed our parents. We simply know our lover is about to move on to greener pastures any day now.

We've all been there.

But for some individuals, it just takes one more situation, one that appears to everyone else as something very trivial indeed, to turn an ordinary, everyday frustration into a totally overwhelming one. Pushed over the edge and feeling there's no way to redeem themselves, they simply want to disappear. For many of the 100,000 reported cases of missing persons in Canada each year, such a scenario might apply. All they needed was a little time to regroup, gain perspective and re-enter their lives with a healthier viewpoint.

For others, the choice to disappear for a longer time— maybe forever—is the only way to cope. Most often these individuals don't blame anyone for their choices. They don't go around saying that the people in their previous lives were the reason they moved on. Instead, they acknowledge that their life circumstances had become more than they could adequately cope with and that something had to give. ∽

TIM MAGEAU

That's exactly what happened in the case of a young man named Tim Mageau.

In 1998, when Tim was 27 years old, he travelled from British Columbia to Toronto to take in a family reunion. An article in the *Toronto Sun* dated September 5, 2003, explained how the young man and his mother, Sharon Paquette, sat down for a long talk before he left to return home to Vancouver, and Tim explained "how he had to get away on his own for awhile." Sharon understood and gave her son the space he needed. But when he didn't call on Mother's Day in 1998, and her efforts to contact him only resulted in a disconnected phone, she did what any concerned mother would do—she flew to Vancouver to see her son in person. And when she found his apartment vacant and learned no one knew of his whereabouts, she was more than a little concerned. It wasn't like her son to disappear like this.

However, there was no reason to believe he'd met with foul play, either. For police, Tim Mageau was an adult who had the perfect right to disappear if he chose to.

Nonetheless determined to make an official missing person's report, Sharon provided police with all the particulars required to identify her son. It took two years of persistence before that official report was filed. Finally, Sharon could rest assured that her son's name had been added to the Canadian Police Information Centre's national database, which could be accessed by law enforcement officials across the country.

Or so she thought. In actual fact, some type of administrative glitch occurred, and Tim's name was not entered until 2003, after Sharon herself had discovered the error. Once it was rectified, her son's name popped up as a witness in a 2002 vandalism report in Calgary. Having lost five years by this time, Sharon wasn't about to sit back and wait another minute. She boarded a plane to the Alberta city and, after pleading her case to a couple of police officers there, they agreed to contact her son. She had finally made the headway she needed to be reunited with her son. But police would only reunite the pair if her son agreed. And he did.

No words were necessary for the mother and son who embraced that day for the first time in what Sharon's way of thinking seemed like a very long time. All was forgiven. The mother and son promised to keep in touch. And Sharon happily boarded a plane back to Toronto, secure in the knowledge that her son was alive and well.

The *Toronto Sun* news story that ran that day, Friday, September 5, 2003, reported that Tim's disappearance didn't have anything to do with his mother or other family members. He just needed to "get away from it all." In this kind of case, a need to get away from it all might translate into a break from routine—a weekend at the beach, a Caribbean cruise, or maybe a week of peace and solitude holed up at home. Since it's commonly said that a change is often as good as a rest, perhaps a move to another apartment or the purchase of a new home is in order. Maybe a new job is the impetus you need to achieve the fresh start you were seeking. Whatever the reason, in some cases, what began as a severing of communication for a few days or weeks goes on until reconnecting doesn't seem possible. Fear of reprisal seems overwhelming and, in all reality, would put you back in the same old rut you tried to escape from in the first place. And so you decide to go "missing" for a while, even if you do so subconsciously. ∾

EVELYN VANDERKRABBEN

Such was the case of Evelyn Vanderkrabben.

By all accounts, Evelyn enjoyed moving from place to place and trying her hand at new opportunities. Her mother, Marian Neill, was well aware of that fact and accepted her daughter's choices. But no matter how transient Evelyn was, she always kept in touch with family and friends. In April 2005, after almost two years of not hearing from her daughter or being able to make contact her, Marian filed a missing person's report with the Durham Regional Police.

"I needed to know if she was alive…if she was alive and happy but didn't want to see us I was okay with that," she told the *Toronto Sun* in May 2005.

After another article about the missing woman appeared in a Durham-area newspaper, Marian was the most hopeful she'd been in a long time. The articles did the trick. A friend of her daughter's noticed Evelyn's story in the Durham-area newspaper and called Evelyn about the matter. Because Evelyn was expecting a child, she knew she couldn't put off contacting her mother any longer. Her child needed a grandma, and she missed her mother.

For Evelyn, there were no bad feelings between herself and her family members, and reconnecting was always something she'd planned to do, but each passing day made it all that much harder for her to consider making contact. It's not an uncommon scenario.

In some cases, a reported missing person wants to remain estranged from their family and friends. In a *Washington Post* article dated March 24, 2006, several women who claimed to be victims in a violent relationship reportedly used Hurricane Katrina as their opportunity to get away and begin a new life for themselves by allowing their names to remain on missing persons' lists. In other cases, disappearing and starting life anew elsewhere becomes a habitual behaviour. ❧

Alma May Gillespie

Such appears to be the case for Alma Mae Gillespie. On more than one occasion she'd disappear, sometimes for years at a time, only to turn up again somewhere in Canada or the U.S. On June 10, 1996, Alma went missing once again, this time from her Winnipeg residence on Edison Avenue. She has not been heard from since. The fact that both her purses were recovered from her apartment gives those who knew and cared for Alma further cause for worry. Her case remains open.

Loved ones who worry about the missing person in their lives deal with a vast array of emotions, ranging from fear and anxiety to outright anger that someone was fine and didn't call home. When asked, most would likely say the same thing—they want to know that the person is okay. A phone call, voice mail, hand-scrawled message or a full-fledged letter, that's all it would take to make a difference. Of course, there are other reasons some people choose to go missing and remain that way. ∾

On the Run

Saturday, July 12, 1997, started out like any other sunny summer day. While some residents of the northern British Columbia community of Kitimat were planning their holidays down south, others were hosting family and friends who'd decided to spend their summer vacations in Kitimat. And why not? Nestled alongside the Douglas Channel, fishing in this neck of the woods is pretty darn good. If smoked salmon doesn't make your mouth water, and you're not into catch and release, there's always the abundance of hiking trails and sights, such as Moore Creek Falls and Humphrey Creek Falls, all ready to provide an abundance of pristine scenery worthy of several rolls of film.

Of course, the younger crowds who've spent the better part of the last school year away from home attending college tend to migrate back to the family nest, taking refuge from rental obligations and looking to make a fast buck at Alcan's aluminum smelter, Eurocan's pulp and paper operation or anywhere else they can find summer employment. Still, it's not all work and no play. Put youth and summer together, and there's got to be some fun in the mix.

That's exactly what Michael Mauro, David Nunes, Donny Oliveira and Mark Teves were looking forward to that weekend—a little time to kick back, catch up with a few old friends and take in a few rays...or so they thought. But before the sun set on this fine summer day, the entire region would be shocked by the news of three dead young men and a fourth hanging on to life by little more than a thread of hope.

Enter Kevin Louis Vermette.

Not much of a people person by most accounts, Vermette liked to keep to himself. Born in 1954, Vermette had called the Kitimat Motel home for several years, and those who knew him described him as an orderly person who was meticulously neat, a brilliant carpenter, a mechanic with a keen interest

in classic cars and so adept in the outdoors he'd put most surviv-
alists to shame. A report in Kitimat's newspaper *The Northern
Sentinel* dated July 16, 1997, pointed to a gentle side to Vermette's personality when a friend was quoted as saying that the
man he knew was also "kind, thoughtful and generous." Certainly, none of these characteristics described the type of person
who could commit the heinous acts of a few days earlier...but
something in him must have snapped.

Information gathered by police led them to believe an
argument between Teves and Vermette allegedly began months
before, when Vermette joined the same gym frequented by Teves
and his buddies. Apparently, the two argued about the loud
music the younger group was playing, and this seemingly insignificant altercation led to a second argument sometime later
that resulted in Vermette actually hitting Teves.

One might think that by now such a mundane disagree-
ment would have accelerated to its limits and then dissipated.
Apparently not. On the morning of July 12, Vermette found
two of his truck's tires slashed and, according to *The Northern
Sentinel,* Vermette immediately came to the conclusion it had to
be the work of Teves and his three friends. Kitimat Motel owner
and manager Murdo MacDonald told reporters he had chatted
with Vermette that morning and, recognizing how angry Vermette was, spent a considerable amount of time trying to calm
him down. By the end of their conversation, Vermette seemed to

do just that—calm down. News that he had, in fact, exploded, hit MacDonald like a bullet in the gut.

Sometime after Vermette's conversation with his landlord, he is believed to have followed Teves, Mauro, Nunes and Oliveira out of town and down to the Hirsch Creek campground. Although Vermette had made threats of bodily harm before, none of the four young men had taken him seriously. Maybe that's why, according to a later account by Oliveira, Vermette was able to get out of his truck, shotgun in hand, and fire off the series of rounds that left Teves, Mauro and Nunes dead and Oliveira clinging to life. No one in Kitimat would have believed Vermette capable of such extreme actions, and the young victims likely never knew what hit them.

Aside from reports of a man leaving the scene in an older model red truck, waving as he went by, no signs of the alleged perpetrator of this bizarre attack were found. While police raced to the Kitimat Motel and surrounded Vermette's room, the man who was wanted for the triple murder and an attempted murder had long since vanished. Wanted posters were plastered throughout the northwest and in other parts of BC within a few days. Detailed descriptions of Vermette's numerous tattoos were made public, along with his personal habits and preferences. And nearly two dozen investigators combed the area, even going so far as to check railway traffic.

The media madness and police public relations efforts over the case brought in hundreds of tips, and Vermette was reported to be spotted in numerous communities across Canada and the United States. In June 1998, almost a year after the attacks, RCMP hoped the announcement of a $17,500 reward for information leading to Vermette's capture would bring in more information. An impassioned plea begging Vermette to turn himself in was written by his mother Alma and printed in the June 10 issue of *The Northern Sentinel* and read by his brother Melvin at the RCMP press conference announcing the reward.

The case was aired in July 2004 and again in July 2005 on FOX TV's hit show *America's Most Wanted,* but to date, not a shred of evidence has provided a solid clue to his whereabouts.

The story of the murders of Teves, Mauro and Nunes, and the attempted murder of Oliveira is occasionally the topic of coffee shop conversation in Kitimat and other towns and villages throughout the northwest. Armchair detectives toss out their own theories on what became of Vermette. At times he's been compared to Alberta's "Mad Trapper of Rat River" and given almost superhuman traits that would enable him to withstand freezing temperatures, survive potentially lethal encounters with wildlife and thrive in the wilderness. Some folks think he may have ended his own life because of the remorse he felt for his actions. Still others reason he may have been ravaged by a bear. Either way, Vermette is listed as a missing fugitive and will likely remain that way for several decades until he's either discovered, turns himself in or dies. In any case, the loner who looked to prefer his own company to that of others will most certainly spend the rest of his life just that way, alone. And as with any other missing person's story, police hope time will bring about the recovery of the missing individual—but in this case, what would await Kevin Vermette would be anything but a welcome-home party.

Chapter Thirteen

Please Tell Me Who I Am

Sometimes the world seems a very small place indeed, such as on those occasions when you take a trip thousands of kilometres away from home and bump into your next-door neighbour at a tourist trap. Other times, your own backyard seems overwhelmingly large. The latter is more a parallel to the way family and friends of a missing person feel—their loved one might be lost, hiding or in some kind of danger in any of a million locations. The search, in such a case, is overwhelmingly large. But what happens when the remains of a John or Jane Doe is discovered? How do investigators identify these individuals, and by doing so, if nothing else, give their families the small comfort of closure?

According to a consultation paper compiled by the Policing, Law Enforcement and Interoperability Branch of Public Safety and Emergency Preparedness Canada, in March 2005, as many as 30 complete or partial sets of human remains are discovered somewhere in the country each year. Not all are victims of foul play. Some of these individuals died as the result of an accident or suicide or succumbed to natural causes. Others are indeed victims of crime. Some of these unidentified remains are recognized and claimed. Others remain John or Jane Does for many years. As of 2005, 286 sets or partial sets of human remains were on record at the Canadian Police Information Centre (CPIC). A number, the report says, that stays fairly consistent from year to year.

The mysteries that follow begin with the discovery of human remains—and that's as far as the story goes. How these people found themselves in a particular location, when, why and how they died are all, for the most part, unknown, along with the most important piece of the puzzle—their identity. ∾

ROSTHERN, SASKATCHEWAN

On Highway 11, nestled between the North and South Saskatchewan rivers almost exactly midway between Saskatoon and Prince Albert, is the community of Rosthern. According to the 2000 Census, Rosthern has a population of about 1500. Not a lot of serious crime happens down in this neck of the woods. In fact, aside from the normal bump and grind of daily life, it's typically peaceful in these parts. So when on May 26, 1982, a farmer checking his cattle along the riverbed near Batoche noticed a body floating in the nearby South Saskatchewan River, there was cause for great alarm.

What Rosthern RCMP found when they arrived at the site was a badly decomposed body of a man who, though he'd been in the river for some time, was remarkably well preserved. Constable Kelly West of the Saskatoon RCMP Major Crimes Unit explained that the man was bald and that his face was undistinguishable. He wasn't wearing a shirt, but he had two pair of pants on—well-worn blue jeans with the back packets missing and a pair of corduroys. Both pair were held up by their own size 34 belts, one of which was a Caswell-brand money belt. The cowboy boots he was wearing were also worn and tattered.

Judging from the condition of his clothes, he could have been a hard-working man. Was he a farmer from around the Rosthern area? Was he just passing through, a construction worker or trucker perhaps? Or had the river transported the body from an altogether different location? He was also wearing a full set of dentures, suggesting he was an individual who was inclined to take care of his health and had the means to do so—or at least he had at one time. Perhaps he was a little down on his luck of late?

The body was transported to Saskatoon, where an autopsy estimated the man's age at between 35 and 40 years. The medical examiner noted that the second and eighth ribs were fractured, but it was believed these injuries were caused by hitting rocks or river ice. And although foul play was pretty much ruled out, the cause of death could not be definitively determined.

Besides a money belt, no identification was recovered from the scene, and the man's identity remained a mystery. Rosthern RCMP had absolutely no clue about the identity of their John Doe. After a long, cold winter, thoughts of who the deceased man could be must have plagued locals.

Information on the Rosthern discovery was immediately sent to the Saskatoon Police Service, which then reviewed reports of missing persons in their files. An incident from the previous November garnered some interest. Apparently on the 27th of that month, someone reported seeing a person jump from the University Bridge. Investigators immediately scoured the river by boat and combed the shoreline on foot. No evidence of a body was discovered.

John Doe's particulars were also sent to the CPIC, which is procedure for any case of missing persons or unidentified remains found in the country, and compared with reports they had on file. The story was also covered in the *RCMP Gazette*—a magazine published by the RCMP and distributed to detachments and police stations across Canada. Nothing concrete came of the nationwide distribution, however, and John Doe's body was interred at Saskatoon's Woodlawn Cemetery, marked with a cement headstone that bore the number 38614. For a time, all that remained to tell of his plight was a cold case file.

In April 2004, two Historical Case Units were established in RCMP "F" Division—one in Regina and the other in Saskatoon. These units are responsible for five categories of cases: homicides, suspicious deaths, missing persons, missing persons where foul play is suspected and found unidentified human remains. That's when Constable Kelly West was first assigned the case of the Rosthern John Doe.

"I contacted Dr. Ernest Walker, forensic anthropologist with the University of Saskatchewan, to discuss the exhumation of the body for re-examination," West said, adding that Dr. Walker is also a Supernumerary Special Constable with the RCMP with 25 years' experience examining crime scenes.

"On July 19, 2004, the body of John Doe was exhumed. All contents of the body bag were examined. Dr. Walker retrieved some bone elements for further examination including the cranium, the mandible, the right pubic bone and three right rib segments. He also retrieved pubic hair for DNA analysis."

Techniques in forensic anthropology had developed considerably over the previous two decades, and John Doe's remains were re-examined to better establish the age, height and build of this unknown soul. The new autopsy revealed some new information. It determined Rosthern's John Doe was a Caucasian of stocky build between 40 and 50 years old at the time of his death, measuring between 177 centimetres (5 feet 10 inches) and 182 centimetres (6 feet) in height. Armed with these new findings, Constable West conducted another check of the CPIC, searching for reports of missing men born between 1930 and 1942.

West then contacted Sergeant Michel Fournier, a forensic artist stationed in "J" Division (New Brunswick), providing him with a detailed report of the investigation, photographs, a description of the clothing the deceased was wearing, the original autopsy report and Dr. Walker's new findings, along with John Doe's cranium and mandible. On October 5, 2005, a photo of the facial reconstruction of the Rosthern John Doe was released to the Saskatoon media. Finally, after more than 20 years, this unknown man once again had a face. From coast to coast, new tips poured in, propelling the investigation forward for a time and providing a renewed hope that a family would get the answers they'd long been looking for. Unfortunately, none of those tips provided a confirmed identity.

"As of right now, the Rosthern John Doe's grave is marked by a cement cylinder with the number 38614 engraved on it," West said. "No one should be remembered as just a number.

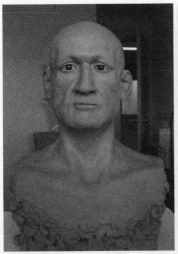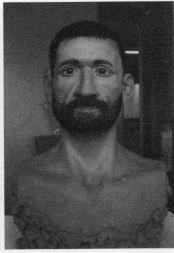

John Doe, Rosthern, SK. Remains found May 26, 1982.

My job is to make all efforts to ensure that will not be the case and that a name will eventually take the place of the number."

The case is still active, and the facial reconstruction so meticulously prepared remains on the national RCMP website, The Doe Network website and the Saskatchewan Association of Chiefs of Police website in the hope that someday, somewhere, somehow, someone will recognize the image and identify the man. Perhaps from there, RCMP can then unravel the mystery of why he ended up floating down the South Saskatchewan River those many years ago. ◈

DICKIE HOVEY AND JOHN DOE BALSAM LAKE

Rocks and trees and a land of lakes, Ontario may have some of Canada's most populated cities, but the province also boasts a plethora of outdoor recreational activities. In late spring or early summer, the area of Balsam Lake Provincial Park starts drawing the first of its summer crowds looking for pristine beaches to laze on, hiking trails to conquer or the first catch of bass of the season to fry. So it is today. So it was back in 1967.

Yet despite the typically high volume of people attracted to the area, it wasn't until December 17, 1967, that the skeletal remains of a young man, thought to have been murdered in the area sometime around June of that year, were discovered in a wooded area just south of Highway 48 near Coboconk.

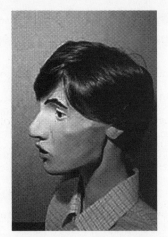 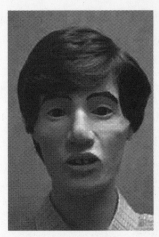

John Doe, Balsam Lake, ON. Remains found December 17, 1967.

An examination of the remains estimated the young man to be anywhere from 15 to 22 years of age, of slight build, and of relatively short stature at 160 centimetres (5 feet 3 inches). His teeth were in good condition. His hair well kept, light brown and about 7.6 centimetres (3 inches) long, but aside from a pair of sized seven Czechoslovakian-made tennis shoes, no clothes were recovered from the scene.

Unique to this case was the 13th thoracic vertebra and a 13th right rib—most humans have 12 thoracic vertebrae and 24 ribs (12 ribs on each side). Whether the individual or his family knew of this anomaly is uncertain, but the irregularity could prove to be an important factor in identifying the young man. And though the cause of death has not been determined, foul play is most definitely suspected in this case—the young man was found with his hands bound behind his back.

Skip ahead to May 1968. During a routine check of a Schomberg-area farm, Beverley Wray's farmhand noticed something out of place. As he was nearing a wire fence outlining the property, the farmhand soon realized what it was he had spotted—the rotting remains of a young man. Investigators of the day placed the deceased's time of death at late spring or early summer the year before. As with the Balsam Lake John Doe, no clothing was discovered in the vicinity of this second victim. He was about 166 centimetres tall (5 feet 5 inches) and of slight build. And his hands were bound behind his back.

That the discovery of these two young men and their subsequent fate were linked back in the mid-1960s is possible. At about the same time, two other young men had been picked up in neighbouring Toronto and were transported and attacked in rural areas. The perpetrator in those cases was eventually apprehended and sentenced, and after being released from that initial prolonged jail term, he reoffended. He was again charged, tried and sentenced to a term of 25 years. Some sources have suggested a link between this individual and the person responsible for the two sets of human remains discovered in the mid-1960s.

In the meantime, in November 2006, the Ontario Provincial Police were just a few months into unveiling a new website called the Resolve Initiative. It was developed to assist law enforcement officials in solving all manner of cold cases including those of missing persons and unidentified remains in the province. Both the files on the two men were reopened and facial reconstructions were created and publicized. Although it has been said that time heals all wounds, and the 40 years between the discoveries of these two sets of unidentified remains and their appearance on the Resolve Initiative website is a very long time indeed, it doesn't necessarily let people forget. Tips immediately began pouring in from people who had long-time missing family members, and by December 19, 2006, the young man discovered in the Schomberg-area farmer's field was identified through a relative and subsequent DNA match as Richard "Dickie" Hovey. Now that police had an identity to work with, they could piece together the jigsaw puzzle of the last few days of his life.

According to his family, Dickie Hovey was just 17 when he set out from his home in New Brunswick in 1967 to travel west to the great metropolis of Toronto. He travelled light—a backpack with a few necessities and a personalized Sears-brand guitar. He was out to make his mark as a musician, something that drew many similarly inclined youngsters to Toronto nightclubs during what was then commonly referred to as the "Summer of Love." Could it be that Dickie Hovey had fallen victim to the same perpetrator charged with other crimes in the area? And what of the young man discovered near Balsam Lake? Although tips have trickled in about this case as well, a confirmed identity has yet to be made. Still, investigators are digging deep, working hard to clear up as many loose ends as possible. After all, in cases dating back four decades, time is of the essence. ∾

Jane Does, Cobourg and Vaughan

Maybe it's because Cobourg boasts a "rare combination of history, natural beauty and community spirit" that it dubs itself "Ontario's Feel Good Town," but a cursory visit to the community of 18,000 is enough to convince even the most jaded newcomer of its charms. The town boasts an historic walking tour of the area sure to tantalize visitors with its stately mansions, historic landmarks and architecture reminiscent of Dickensian London. Whether you kick off your shoes and sink your feet into the sandy shoreline of Cobourg's beach, take in the many shops or just sit a spell at one of the town's many cafés or eating establishments, Cobourg definitely has a lot to offer.

By November 9, 2002, Thanksgiving celebrations were merely a memory, and folks were starting to gear up for the coming Christmas season. For some diehard outdoors people, the holiday season wouldn't be complete without fresh game to celebrate, and on this day hunters were combing the Northumberland Forest north of town for just that—a tasty treat to tempt the missus with. The first two weeks of November spell deer season in these parts. But the doe these hunters discovered wasn't of the four-legged variety. What they came across was the unidentified remains of a woman.

Even after an initial investigation, there are many questions about the Jane Doe of Northumberland Forest that remain unanswered. Estimates place her between 30 and 50 years of age, though her probable height, weight, overall build, and hair and

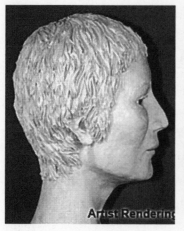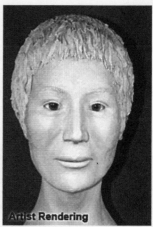

Jane Doe, Cobourg, ON. Remains found November 9, 2002.

eye colour are uncertain. A detailed examination of her teeth revealed she'd had dental work in the past, but that in the years immediately preceding her death she'd suffered from two severe dental abscesses. Her cause of death remains unknown.

To the west and slightly north of Cobourg is the City of Vaughan. Incorporated in 1991, Vaughan proudly refers to itself as "The City Above Toronto." Located on the northwestern corner of the Ontarian metropolis, Vaughan is dubbed as one of southern Ontario's fastest-growing cities; Statistics Canada reported its population had increased by a remarkable 37.3 percent between 1996 and 2001. In terms of numbers, in 2001 the city's population was recorded at 182,022, up almost 50,000 persons from the 1996 figure of 132,549. An increase in population

requires more of life's amenities—more daycare, schooling, recreational facilities, health care provisions, infrastructure and so
on. And sadly, more people usually mean more crime.

Still, there are some areas surrounding Vaughan that
speak to the centre of agriculture it once was. When hunting
season comes around, those so inclined still scout the city's
perimeter for pheasant, northern bobwhite, wild turkey or other
game. It was just such an occasion that led four hunters to
a wooded area in the city's Pine Valley Drive area just before
Christmas 2002. With eyes peeled for any signs of a camou-
flaged partridge, coon or possum, the hunters were keenly aware
of their surroundings. That's when they stumbled upon what
was later determined to be another type of hunter's prey—the
skeletal remains of a young woman. Not a nice sight at any time
of the year, and a particularly distressful one to discover two
days before Christmas. Someone would receive some distressing
news instead of the seasonal yuletide joy. The problem was that
with little more to go on than bone, discovering the identity of
the deceased wouldn't be easy.

Members of the Archeological Forensic Recovery Unit
of the York Regional Police scoured the area, collecting as
much of the skeleton as they could find. Back in the laboratory,
they determined their victim was a young Caucasian woman
between the ages of 18 and 20 years. Her teeth appeared to be in
good shape, but that wasn't necessarily true of the rest of her
body. Her nose, ribs and vertebrae all showed signs of healed

Jane Doe, Vaughan, ON. Remains found December 23, 2002.

fractures, and another injury suggested that the decedent had been a victim of foul play. Further examination of the remains indicated that the victim had met with her fate between one and three years earlier. With such a considerable time lapse between death and discovery, it's no wonder little else was discovered to help provide investigators with clues. The only other piece of evidence uncovered was a single, silver barbell—a piece of jewellry most commonly used in body piercing of the tongue or eyebrow.

Using what physical information police had available, a facial reconstruction was made and photographs were circulated to law enforcement agencies across the country.

To date, no information of any significance on either of the above cases has been uncovered, but both remain open. ∾

DYERS BAY, BRUCE PENINSULA, ONTARIO

If you're into water sports, sunbathing or pristine wilderness hikes, Bruce Peninsula has just about everything you're looking for. Located on the world-renowned Niagara Escarpment, the park is home to seven nature reserves and two national parks. It's hard to imagine that on August 10, 2005, with an idyllic backdrop where folks enjoy the summer sun and all seems very good with the world, that not so very far away in a rugged wooded campsite the remains of an adult male were discovered.

To be precise, skeletal remains of what appeared to belong to a man aged 20 to 50 years were found northeast of the Junction of Dyers Bay Road and Highway #6, almost midway between Wiarton and Tobermory. An examination of the remains revealed the individual was a Caucasian, about 182 centimetres (6 feet) tall and weighing about 200 pounds (90 kilograms).

It's always a bonus when, in such a macabre discovery as this, personal items are also uncovered, and here the unknown victim did not disappoint, at least not initially. Several assorted personal items were found, some of which initially looked to be promising clues to the deceased's identity. A zippered, blue jacket that bore a "Canada Post" logo and a "Made in Canada" tag with the insignia "Canada Post Corporation," along with a similarly-made blue vest also sporting a "Canada Post" logo, both sized 3X, were found near the body. But it was later discovered that the owner of the vest had donated it to a social service agency in Langley, BC, back in 2001, closing off the possibility that the current owner had been a postal worker.

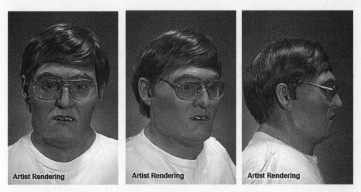

John Doe, Dyers Bay, Bruce Peninsula, ON. Remains found August 10, 2005.

A hunting knife with the initials "EH" engraved on the chrome butt of its black handle was also discovered, along with a pair of eyeglasses and sunglasses, a cigarette tin and assorted personal items and camping gear—a cache of goods, really, but nothing that might provide concrete evidence as to the identity of the deceased.

What the gent was doing in the area, who he was and what he died of are all still mysteries police are determined to solve. ❧

HALIFAX INTERNATIONAL AIRPORT, HALIFAX, NOVA SCOTIA

Like any other international airport in Canada, Nova Scotia's Halifax International is a busy place. Whether they're coming or going, passengers in the hectic airport numbered 3,242,389 in 2004. The flow of passengers represented a huge increase from the 180,000 or so using the facility when it first opened for business in 1960, and business continues to grow.

Oddly enough, the best place to get lost is in a crowd. It's not like people don't notice what's happening around them, but there's so much going on it's often difficult to interpret and remember everything you see. Regardless, on October 8, 2004, in a wooded area not far from the busy airport, a grizzly discovery was made—a badly decomposed body of a man. It was a discovery that to date remains unsolved, partly because no one seems to have noticed anything out of the ordinary at that time. At least, nothing they were aware of.

Decomposed though the body was, the man's time of death was estimated at about 10 days before his body was discovered. This fairly short time frame gave investigators at least something of a guideline for their examination. Although he wasn't wearing any jewellry, it looked as though both his ears were pierced. He wore his hair in medium-length dread-locks and also had a small, well-groomed beard.

The clothing he was wearing, along with other personal items, hinted at the type of person the decedent was before his demise. With a jean-size waist and inseam both measuring 81 centimetres (32 inches), it's safe to say the man was of average build and a little short in the leg. Along with his Lees jeans, the Halifax International Airport's John Doe sported a few other designer labels—an Emilio sweater, Timberland hiking boots, Italian designer Dolce & Gabbana prescription glasses and

a Mckinley backpack. Inside his backpack, other items of clothing were neatly folded, possibly suggesting that this unknown
character was an orderly person who wanted things "just so."

Yet for a fellow with such an apparent bent to all things
particular, it appeared he either hadn't gotten the medical attention he needed for a broken leg or it hadn't properly healed
before the cast was removed.

What is missing—when it comes to information gleaned
from a body or discovery site—is almost as telling as what
remains. This John Doe carried no identification, no airplane
ticket, no illicit drugs or other substances—and unlike what the
suspicious nature of the discovery suggested, there appeared to
be no indication of foul play. So why would a well-dressed, well-
groomed, well-organized fellow drop dead in the middle of
nowhere, and not a soul report him as missing?

A year later, in November 2005, the body was exhumed
for further examination. Forensic anthropologist Dr. Tanya
Peckmann estimated the decedent was about 180 centimetres
(5 feet 11 inches) tall, and weighed 72 kilograms (160 pounds),
indicating the fellow most likely sported an athletic build.
She also suggested he was either Black African or of mixed heritage, possibly of partial European descent, and was somewhere
between the ages of 18 and 23 at the time of his death.

Forensic art specialist Sergeant Michel Fournier was
called in on the case for his expertise in facial reconstruction.

After 120 hours of replicating the skull, bones, facial features and hair, Fournier was able to give the unknown man a face. Photographs were released to the media on November 23, 2006, but as of this writing, the man has still not been identified. ∽

CONCEPTION BAY SOUTH, NEWFOUNDLAND

In May of any given year, the weather down in Conception Bay South, Newfoundland, is known to be unpredictable. It might look as if it's going to be a nice, balmy Victoria Day long weekend, but if you're planning on tenting for your getaway, make sure you pack a few pair of long johns—more often than not you'll go to sleep warm and toasty one night but wake up to a dump of snow the next morning.

The area is also known for giving up its skeletons. The nearby Manuels River System is a natural heritage site, boasting a collection of some of the oldest trilobite⁎fossils in the province. It's not uncommon for folks out for a hike in the area to uncover a few impressions of these prehistoric organisms. Hikers might even find parts of the trilobite's outer shell still attached. But on May 17, 2001, Conception Bay South coughed up the remains of an entirely different species. The skeletal remains of a male between the ages of 20 and 40 were discovered just off Minerals Road.

That Fort Townshend police were dealing with human remains was a given—they had the man's skull and a few other assorted bones to work with. But there was little else, and even an intensive, detailed search of the area produced no additional clues as to who the man was.

An extensive study of what remains were discovered gave investigators a few clues to follow up, however. They were able to determine the age of the man, find dental records and develop a DNA profile. Investigators also concluded that the individual once sported shoulder-length hair, was a victim of a homicide and was "placed" in the area within the last 10 years. Was the unidentified man from Newfoundland or a visitor who found himself in harm's way? Investigators are still searching for answers. ❧

WRAPPING IT UP

Knowing that unidentified human remains were once people with families and friends is what provides law enforcement officials with the impetus to find answers. Although some of these unknown individuals were deemed victims of foul play or suicide, others were simply homeless wanderers who could have died of natural causes.

The cases in this section were ones where reconstructions or artist renderings were completed. Should you be interested, log onto the OPP Resolve Initiative website (http://www.opp.ca/Investigative/UnidentifiedRemains/index.htm), and browse the photographs of other unidentified individuals. Be warned though, many of the pictures may be disturbing.

Chapter Fourteen

So What Is "Missing"?

I t's interesting how family stories are often repeated over and over and yet never really examined for their significance. As I researched and wrote about the people covered in this book, I kept thinking how very lucky our family was that we'd never experienced the disappearance of someone we loved. And then it hit me. Go back a couple of generations and we did have such a scenario.

I never met my maternal grandfather. He died almost a decade before I was born. But if temperament is handed down genetically, and my mother and I are any indication, I'd bet he was a fairly headstrong and determined man in his day. While those qualities can be beneficial in many ways, they can also get you into trouble if you're not careful.

Although I've never travelled to the Ukraine, I don't have to close my eyes to see the scene, as my mother told it. I can picture a cloudy day, the wind tussling with the sprigs of grass and brush in an endless field. I can hear children laughing and playing, carelessly tossing out a joke here, a nasty tease there. Then I can imagine my grandfather, still a boy really at 12 or 13 years, frustrated by the remarks spat out by one of the girls in the group. Impulsively he grabbed a rock and hurled it in her direction. Action before thought. And then the unthinkable happened. The rock hit her head, and she fell to the ground. Horrified at his actions, my grandfather fled—and in a big way. He didn't wait around to find out if the girl was okay. He didn't run home to Mama. He assumed he'd fatally injured his friend, and he was terrified. So he did what any other young lad would do back at the turn of the 20th century. He stowed away on a ship and made his way to Canada.

This book began with the question "what is 'missing'?" Clearly, in my grandfather's case, burdened by what could have been merely imaginary guilt, he didn't think of himself as missing. For my maternal great-grandparents, their son had disappeared, and they never heard from him again. In this case, my grandfather went on to live a relatively happy and productive life. Sadly, that isn't always the case.

Throughout the pages of this book I've told of the many reasons why people may go missing and examine a little of the pain and suffering of those who are left behind worrying and wondering what became of their loved one. Some stories will never be resolved. But if there's one thing I've learned, it's that the glimmer of hope always shines, no matter how dimly, until it is proven that no hope remains. And it is up to all of us to work together to help bring resolution.

So next time you're walking through your local mall, shopping at your grocery store of choice or passing a light post with a missing person's banner on it, take a moment to study the face. Read the brief description and story accompanying it. Commit the information to memory, and stay alert. You never know when you may be the vehicle that ends someone's misery and reunites a family.

Notes on Sources

Information for stories throughout this text was retrieved from numerous sources, including several community news outlets, online and print publications, and special interest groups: *20/20, ABC News, America's Most Wanted, Amnesty International, Calgary Herald, Calgary Sun, Canadian Press, canadianchristianity.com, canadianencyclopedia.ca, Canoe News, CBC News, Child Find Canada, The Coast Halifax's Weekly, CourtTV Crime Library, CourtTV News, CTV News, digitaljournal.com, Doe Network, Doors of Hope, Edmonton Journal, Edmonton Sun, Fifth Estate, The Fountain Pen, FOX News, lastlinkontheleft.com, godutch.com, London Free Press, Manitoulin Expositor, Missing Children Society of Canada, missingpeople.org, National Missing Persons Helpline, North Shore News, Northern Sentinal, NOW Toronto, Oakville Beaver, orato.com, Ottawa Sun, Prince George Free Press, Seattle Times, Smithers Interior News, Someone is Missing: An Emotional Resource for the Family and Friends of Missing Persons, thestar.com, Toronto Mike (www.mikeboon.com), Toronto Sun, vancourier.com, Vancouver 24 Hours, Vancouver Sun, W-FIVE, wikipedia.com, Winnipeg Sun, youtube.com.*

Book Sources

Clarkes, Lincoln. *Heroines.* Vancouver, BC: Anvil Press, 2002.

de Vries, Maggie. *Missing Sarah.* Toronto, ON: Penguin Canada, 2003.

Gledhill, Marilyn and Joe. *Our Son Is Missing, The Story of a Six-Week Nightmare.* Hansport, NS: Lancelot Press, 1996.

Greene, Trevor. *Bad Date, The Lost Girls of Vancouver's Low Track.* Toronto, ON: ECW Press, 2001.

Haines, Max. *True Crime Stories.* Toronto, ON: Key Porter Books Ltd. (Prospero Books), 2003.

Murdoch, Derrick. *Disappearances, True Accounts of Canadians Who Have Vanished.* Toronto, ON: Doubleday Canada Ltd., 1983.

Key Internet Sources

Canadian Centre for Justice Statistics Profile Series, Women in Canada:
http://www.statcan.ca/english/research/85F0033MIE/85F0033MIE2001010.pdf

City of Vancouver 2006 population counts:
http://www.city.vancouver.bc.ca/commsvcs/planning/census/2006/popdwellcounts.pdf

DNA Missing Persons Index Canada:
http://ww2.ps-sp.gc.ca/publications/policing/mpi/index_e.asp#3

Human Trafficking:

http://www.unodc.org/unodc/trafficking_human_beings.html

http://www.justice.gc.ca/en/fs/ht/index.html

http://usinfo.state.gov/xarchives/display.html?p=washfile-english&y=2007&m=March&x=20070308105720ajesrom0.5518

Natel King:

http://www.montcopa.org/da/pressreleases/more%20charges.htm

http://origin-www.aopc.org/OpPosting/Supreme/out/504mal2006.pdf

Lisa and Nickolas Masee:

http://www.leg.bc.ca/hansard/34th2nd/34p_02s_880502p.htm

Prostitution Awareness & Action Foundation of Edmonton:

http://www.paafe.org/Home.html

Ambrose Small:

http://www.russianbooks.org/small.htm

http://www.prairieghosts.com/ambrose.html

http://www.grandtheatre.com/aboutus/history/history.asp

http://www.lib.uoguelph.ca/resources/archives/collection_update/11/11gt/index.html

Other Internet Sources

Durham Regional Police Service: http://www.drps.ca/netscape/index.asp

http://www.forensicartist.com/reconstruction.html

http://www.hockeydraftcentral.com/1984/84020.html

http://www.mapleleafs.com/

http://www.ourmissingchildren.gc.ca/omc/publications/2006/2005MissingChildrenReferenceReport.pdf

Prince George RCMP:
http://www.rcmp-grc.gc.ca/bc/programs/aps/profiles/north/princegeorge_e.htm

Royal Newfoundland Constabulary: http://www.justice.gov.nl.ca/rnc/Startpage.htm

http://www.rcmp-grc.gc.ca/crimint/drugs_2005_e.htm

RCMP Halifax: http://www.rcmp-grc.gc.ca/missing_persons/index_e.htm

York Regional Police: http://www.police.york.on.ca/

Index

Websites on Missing Persons

Note to the Reader:

Unfortunately, only a few photos were available for the many cases mentioned in this book. Because it didn't seem right to have only these few scattered in the body of the work, we have placed these photos in the final pages.

How can someone stand before you one minute, talking and breathing and going through their daily routine, and the next minute disappear? It's a situation we all hope never touches our lives, but it is all too common.

Stories of missing persons so captured the imagination of Angela Ellis that in 1999 she decided to do something with her concern and formed the Internet database known as the Doe Network.

Jessica ("Jessie") Foster of Kamloops has been missing from Las Vegas since March 2006.

Delphine Nikal went missing from Smithers, BC, in June 1990.

The volunteer-run, non-profit organization lists pages and pages of individuals who've gone missing, complete with their names, photos and stories. It is the network's hope that someone, some-where, might have an answer in one of these cases.

Law enforcement agencies, as well as non-profit groups and families of missing persons have also used the information high-way as a way to get the word out and to garner important infor-mation. Most of the websites listed in this section are living scrapbooks that are added to on a regular basis, so please return to them from time to time. You never know when you might be the key to drawing closure for a grieving family.

The Doe Network: http://www.doenetwork.org/

Jessica Foster: www.jessiefoster.ca

Highway of Tears: http://highwayoftears.ca/news.htm

Missing Native Women: http://www.missingnativewomen.ca/

Missing People: http://www.missingpeople.net/

Ontario Provincial Police Resolve Initiative: http://www.opp.ca/Investigative/UnidentifiedRemains/index.htm

Project KARE: http://www.kare.ca/

Alicia Ross: http://www.aliciaross.ca/alicia/story/

Vancouver's Missing Women: http://www.missingpeople.net/

Fran Young: www.findfran.com

Cecilia Nikal disappeared in 1989, just a year before her cousin Delphine Nikal went missing. Both girls were last seen on the infamous Highway of Tears near Smithers, BC.

About the Author

Lisa Wojna

Lisa Wojna, author of several other non-fiction books, has worked in the community newspaper industry as a writer and journalist and has travelled all over Canada, from the windy prairies of Manitoba to northern British Columbia, and even to the wilds of Africa. Although writing and photography have been a central part of her life for as long as she can remember, it's the people behind every story that are her motivation and give her the most fulfillment.